# DAYS OF FEAR

# DAYS OF FEAR

## DIARY OF A 1920s HUNGER STRIKER

### FRANK GALLAGHER

MERCIER PRESS
WHAT YOU NEED TO READ

MERCIER PRESS
Cork
www.mercierpress.ie

Trade enquiries to CMD Distribution
55A Spruce Avenue, Stillorgan Industrial Park,
Blackrock, County Dublin.


*First published by Mercier Press in 1967 – this edition 2008*

© A. Gallagher
Foreword © Gabriel Doherty, 2008

ISBN: 978 1 85635 586 5

10 9 8 7 6 5 4 3 2 1

A CIP record for this title is available from the British Library

arts
council
schomhairle
ealaíon
Mercier Press receives financial assistance from the Arts
Council/An Chomhairle Ealaíon

Printed and bound by J.H. Haynes & Co. Ltd, Sparkford

# Contents

# FOREWORD

'This book contains what must be one of the strangest diaries ever published.'

The words of the Editorial Note of the 1967 Mercier Press edition of *Days of Fear* are still pertinent now, forty years after that publication and more than eighty-five years after the Mountjoy hunger strike, the course of which is chronicled herein.

The book is indeed strange; it is also, by turns, humorous, insightful, dramatic and poignant. It offers a perspective not just on the day-to-day actions of the principals in the drama – the hunger strikers themselves – but also on the behind-the-scenes machinations that are inescapable features of all such political theatre. It offers valuable insights, further-more, into the mindsets – the oft unspoken and frequently unspeakable hopes, fears and regrets – of the protagonists, not just in the battle within the prison walls but also in the war without.

One cannot have a diary without a diarist, of course, and Frank Gallagher was ideally suited to the role of chronicler-in-chief of those nine traumatic April days. Then in his twenty-seventh year, he was an experienced journalist and a member of that talented generation of literary men (including Seán O'Faoláin and Frank O'Connor) who emerged from the southern capital around this time. Having joined the republican movement in 1917, he found his niche in Dáil Éireann's Propaganda Department (subsequently renamed the Publicity Department) during the War of Independence. During this time, he both left an indelible mark on the *Irish Bulletin*, the department's principal publication, and became sincere friends with Erskine Childers, amongst many others. Arrested in March 1920, his brief sojourn in Mountjoy did little to reduce his appetite for the political fray, and on his release he found himself playing a central role in the republican publicity campaign for the remainder of the war.

His influence on the national scene waned over the following decade because of the defeat of the anti-Treatyite cause to which he gave his support in the Civil War. It waxed afresh, however, as a result of the emergence in 1926 of Fianna Fáil, in whose service he was, in effect, to remain for the rest of his professional life – firstly as de Valera's personal secretary, then as editor of the party journal *The Nation*, subsequently (and most famously) as editor of the *Irish Press*, and with a stint as director of the Government Information Bureau thrown in for good measure. Towards the latter part of his life he turned his hand towards the writing of history (*The Four Glorious Years* (1953), his account of the revolutionary struggle, remains a classic of nationalist historiography) and political commentary (notably *The Indivisible Island* (1957) which was, for many years, the definitive articulation of the anti-partitionist argument).

He was, in short, a significant figure in the first four decades of the independent Irish state, and knowledge of his life and work deserves a wider audience.

This reissue of *Days of Fear,* which was originally published in 1928, will, hopefully, go some way towards achieving this end. It occupies an important position in the small but influential canon of Irish prison writings, itself a subset of an oft-overlooked literary genre. While not as widely-read as John Mitchel's *Jail Journal,* the Irish archetype for such memoirs, it is an impressive piece of work, some of the more interesting elements of which are those which relate the unintentional or darkly humorous moments of the strike, the ruminations on the morality of fasting 'till death and the dramatic mood swings experienced by the prisoners, often, indeed usually, for little or no good reason.

While more academic treatments of the subject exist (the best being Seán McConville's monumental *Irish Political Prisoners, 1848–1922: Theatres of war*), none, I think, has the immediacy and vibrancy of Gallagher's prose. Savour, then, the contents of this short, thought-provoking and, yes, intriguingly *strange* book.

GABRIEL DOHERTY,

SPRING 2008

# Editorial Note

This book contains what must be one of the strangest diaries ever published.

It was written during one of those periodic protests for national liberty in Ireland in which passionate self-sacrifice seems to become the temporary characteristic of a whole people. It is a record of spiritual strength, of reckless suffering, and of frank cowardice – something that all men and women serving an ideal have tasted.

Yet these pages do not stand aloof from any of us. They are poignantly human, as full of gentleness as of fear, as full of despair as they are of faith; and they make the book one that we close with that happiness which brings tears.

Its period is the Hunger-strike in Mountjoy Jail, Dublin, in 1920. At the time this protest by imprisoned men attracted world-wide attention, which had perhaps more to do with the manner of its ending than anything which happened inside the jail. The continental and transatlantic press sent representatives to Dublin to watch its progress.

The day-to-day journal of one who took part in that fast, written during the agony itself, makes at times uncanny reading, yet the truth of its obsessions as well as of its ecstasies becomes very real to us as we turn the pages.

## Easter Monday, April 5th, 1920

There is a queer happiness in me. If it were not so quiet in this cell and in the whole jail, I would sing and call out in sheer gaiety of spirit.

The fight is on, the fight that now can have but one ending ... triumph and freedom, something done for liberty and the rights of all men ... God is good to us. We have got the strength to begin. This day week we shall be back amongst our friends, amongst our people. And proud of us, they will say that we have done well, that we were brave ... There was never such a joy on me as this. I love Ireland and all the world and the courage that is everywhere.

This morning there was misgiving. There is none now ...

The porridge tasted sweet this morning. Perhaps it knew

13

its mission, that it will have to keep us alive until we have won. 'This is the last time you will be washed by me,' I said to the enamel plate, though dear knows there was not much need to wash it at all. 'This is the last time,' I said to the bone translucent spoon as I licked the last fleck of creaminess from it. 'Get ready for your new master,' I told the wooden salt-cellar ...

And then I tried to read Harry Johnston's *Colonisation of Africa* as I waited for the cell doors to be opened for exercise. But my hands were moist with forebodings and the words would not stay in their own lines ... I closed the book and walked up the cell and down, up and down, humming old songs and whistling and saying, 'God, Your help be with us now,' and wondering would it be and trying not to think of the days to come ...

At last the banging of drawn bolts ... the silent passages filled with sharp echoing sounds ... and I was in the open, going down the stone steps to the cage where we exercised, my arm around Peter Starkey's shoulder ... I could have hugged him when I saw the far-off prison wall golden above the green gardens of the hospital. The sun was full upon it. But we had to turn away from that light and pass through the wicket in the ten-foot iron railings which circled the exercise-ring. And the ring was close to the great jail buildings ... in permanent shadow.

Today the prisoners did not, as on other mornings, hurry to where the rag-ball had been hidden the night before, forming themselves into rushing teams and roaring spectators. They stood about in groups, expectantly.

Suddenly Philip, our O/C, called out in his penetrating, unraised voice: 'Now, lads.'

We crowded around him, more than fifty of us ... The doubled sentries outside the cage were listless ... Life, curiosity, came back to them as, Philip's voice leading, a chorus, deep-toned in earnest dedication, swelled up from behind the ten-foot bars:

> I pledge myself to the honour of Ireland and the lives of my comrades not to eat food or drink anything except water until all here have been given prisoner-of-war treatment or are released.

Philip and Twomey and I walked the exercise-ring afterwards, threading our way through the knots and groups of other men, or stepping back suddenly as one of the few who had gone back to the rag-ball hurled himself after it. Philip was radiant. 'Twice as many on hunger-strike as ever before,' he said; 'we'll have the jail gates open by Saturday!'

'I think we're in for a tough time,' I said.

'The tougher the better,' Philip answered. 'The real fight is beginning outside. And' (fiercely) 'I am going to be out for it.'

'Or out *of* it,' Twomey said whimsically.

'No,' Philip said quietly. 'We'll win this time. If we are as hard as iron with ourselves and refuse every compromise, we'll end it in a week. G.H.Q. are going to make things lively outside while we fight them here. It will be only a question of days.'

'All in,' shouted the warder-in-charge.

We trooped back to our cells, joking, jubilant and … each to himself … a little uneasy …

We are launched on an adventure whose end none knows …

Heigh-ho, but you are a harsh taskmaster, Ireland! Ten days ago I was free, walking Dublin's streets. Now I am in this cell, not tried, not charged, yet doomed to fast until I am free again. These be crowded times, surely. Only ten days ago Kirwan and I planned the excursion which has ended thus …

We agreed to forget Ireland for one night, to buy no evening paper, to ignore the war around us, to lose ourselves in a theatre and walk afterwards until we saw the moonlight on Dublin Bay … Not until we had returned to the centre of the city, our faces tingling under the east wind, our steps echoing on pavements jewelled with frost, was our dreaming broken … An old woman running,

16

resting in aged weakness against an area railings, running again … That ended the peace in us. Curfew was at hand. Soon the streets would be of a dead city until the military lorries began the nightly hunt for prisoners …

The first I knew of that day's tragedy was when I entered the sitting-room of my lodgings. The other boarders were British in their sympathies. Tonight they were sullen and did not greet me. Something dark had happened. One by one they went stiffly, silently to bed, I drew in my chair to the leaping fire. Louie was reading a novel. My eyes searched the room for an evening paper. There was one on the floor. I hesitated before bending for it, for to read it meant conversation and … Louie would not understand. She had not said, 'Goodnight, Gally,' when I came in, nor poked the fire for me. Whatever news that paper contained had hardened her … At last I picked it up … The fire made a pleasant, roaring noise in the silent room …

Without looking up from her book, Louie said: 'You don't stand for that, Gally, do you?' … There was supplication in her voice.

Alan Bell, I told her, though an old man, was the agent of the tyranny we were fighting. If his age should have shielded him against the swift, hard death he met that morning, then it should have made innocent that Kaiser for whose hanging she herself had longed with such intensity.

17

I did not believe in assassination, but injustice bred cruel children. Britain had suppressed every other expression of our nationality except the gun … I was on the defensive …

She read her book again and the pleasant burr of the fire filled the silent room.

Before that other noise came out of the night we had forgotten the war and were talking pleasantly of things of no account … Suddenly Louie raised her voice ever so slightly. I knew then that she had heard it also, and understood its meaning. It was the sound of a military lorry coming towards the house …

The pretence that there was no sound outside became ridiculous and we stopped talking … The lorry halted a few feet from our lighted window … We stood, waiting for the thunderous knocking … After an aeon of silence the engine of the lorry was restarted and it drove away …

'Yet, I almost knew it was for you, Gally,' Louie said softly.

'I also,' I answered.

… And it was for me …

Two hours later I woke, conscious of being trapped. The room was dark. The house was very still. I held my breath, listening … There was not a sound … not a … Then just outside the door I heard creeping steps … a hand

eerily feeling the surface of the door for the door-knob …
I thought of Thomas MacCurtain, Lord Mayor of Cork,
assassinated in his home in revenge for a British constable. What would be the price of Alan Bell, a Dublin Castle
official? …

The gliding hand found the handle … Out of the blackness the bedclothes blazed suddenly about me … The long
nose of a Webley shone like a silver pencil in the broad-
ening ray. I waited for the revolver to speak, not in fear
or with thought of danger, but with unbearable curiosity,
with yearning that the silence might end … Then something in me said: 'Don't shout when hit' … Subconsciously
I noticed the flash of a bayonet in the void behind the
torch, like a fish turning in a dark pool … Why were they
so quiet? Why did they not fire or something? Why was
that deadly silver pencil so still and straight? … Somebody
whispered … a hand rubbed along the wall and found the
electric switch …

'Frank Gallagher?'

'Yes.'

'Dress; we want you.'

… The dawn was lightening the night sky when at last
the questionings and searchings were over … The escort
formed about me as I reached the tiled hall … The street-
door swung open. 'March,' barked the young officer. I heard

Louie's voice: 'Take care of him now,' and the official reply: 'Yes, madam!' The dawn wind was cold. As the lorry moved from the house a cry came over the sound of the throbbing engine: 'Good-bye, Gally.' It brings a lump to my throat even now ...

## TUESDAY, APRIL 6TH, 1920

Tonight my head aches ... Those first days of hunger-striking are cruel days. Yet the hardest thing of all to bear is that there are no meal-hours. Jail life hinges on the three meals. It is morning, and one is brisk and vigorous because the tin at the door has porridge in it. It is afternoon, and a calm studiousness invades the mind because the contents of that tin are soup and potatoes. It is drowsy evening, and one begins to yawn because soup and potatoes have given way to cocoa and crusted bread ... And now there is no division of the day, no beginning and no end ... The head aches, the body is damp and weak ... even sleep has gone.

Today in the exercise-ring it was queer. Men who two days ago laughed and shouted and plunged after that rag-ball now slouched along, trying once or twice to pretend that it was all a joke, to skip and run and – fall back into listlessness ... There was a gloom coming upon us all ... And then ...

Then the news came from outside, rapturous news, news of victory! Four years ago, at Easter time, the Irish had re⁻belled. Therefore, to the official mind Easter time is rebellion time. And for this Easter troops were poured into the cities, tanks waddled in their wake. Every staff officer said to every subaltern: 'Leave nothing to chance.' And nothing was left to chance. Dublin was ringed round with barbed wire, bar⁻ricades of soldiers held all entrances to the city and all exits. Patrols marched the coast roads, watching for landings of arms. Military posts, established at every street corner, their tin hats cutting the dawn sky and the sunset, waited for the rebels to march in long defiant columns through the main streets ... and while they waited a few Irishmen in each city, at the same hour in all parts of the nation, gathered silently and suddenly around the doors of two hundred constabulary barracks and tax-collectors' offices and, forcing an entrance, burned them to the ground ...

The news changed the exercise-ring from a morgue to a marriage feast. The slouchers walked with their shoulders back and called to one another: 'We have them on the run, boys' ... The certainty of success came back ... We forgot our aching heads and the queer feeling inside us ...

The thought has just come lividly to me that, in

announcing my resolve a week ago to hunger-strike on my own, I precipitated this protest ... What if it should fail ... horribly?

# WEDNESDAY, APRIL 7TH, 1920

Not many in the exercise-ring this morning … Philip was there and Twomey. Philip's clear-cut face becomes more angular with his fast. Twomey's easy bulk remains unchanged, eyes just a little brighter.

Talked, as quietly we went round the ring like old horses ready for the knacker's blow. Philip's buoyancy is flaming still. Twomey cited the news brought in by the latest prisoners of more assassinations of Republican leaders in the South. 'That's a temper the Castle never showed before,' he said. 'It won't be so easy as you think, Philip.'

We walked our careful walk in silence.

Philip said suddenly: 'Hunger-striking is different. They don't know how to meet it. Ashe died after four days of it and the dread of unexpected deaths has been over the British since. They never know when one of us will go. Late last night young Mitchel fainted in his cell. The Governor was told, and lost his nerve. He thought it was the first of a regiment of deaths. They raced Mitchel over to the hospital and called three doctors.'

We walked silently for a little while … I was thinking of young Mitchel as he fainted …

Philip said again: 'I admit the Castle would gladly shoot us all out of hand if they got the chance. But letting us die by inches frightens them. Believe me, Twomey, they'll cave in as soon as they see we're in earnest. Not one of us has been charged or tried. They have no excuse for holding us until we die …'

We walked our slow walk.

A minute or two before the warders herded us in, twelve new prisoners, fresh and rosy-faced from the country districts, tramped into the ring. Philip went towards them at once.

'Well, boys – ' he began.

'We are all on strike,' said the tall, lean man who led them, laughing at the way he had forestalled Philip's appeal. Philip's eyes beamed from his hard face.

'It's glorious,' he said to me as we climbed the stone stairs. 'Twenty yesterday, twelve today. All army men and all into the strike the moment they reach the jail.'

I felt for them … the first days are so miserable …

With us, the old-stagers, this life without meals is

becoming normal. There is much less pain in the head. The sense of fragile emptiness is wearing away ... Sometimes a rush of hot, clammy fear, a racing of the heart ... a prayer. Then smoothness again, weariness without pain ... subconscious waiting for the next sudden storm ... And, greatest of all, a fierce joy, a sacrificial glory, a feeling of spiritual pride ... an ecstasy ...

Read Harry Johnston until the light died out of the cell ... Felt an unspeakable pity for these rude peoples who come so suddenly under an Empire's harrow ... the cruelty of all empires! The dead they leave by the wayside ... the numbed hearts ... the desolate un-understanding homes ... huts of grass with no light in them save the whites of eyes waiting for the next blow ... barbarous, never-ending injustice against which even anger is pitiable ... All empires are the same ... ruthless ... efficient ... completely soulless ... incapable of understanding. One wants to cry ...

But, brothers of Africa, we whom you know not of are making one empire weaker ...

If one could feel that somewhere in these dark, twilit forests there was even one village where the white man would never come, and where the hushed peace would never be broken and the little daily round go on of rude and gentle savage life, so much more gentle than the coming of the pioneers of civilisation, with their slave-gangs and their treacheries and their trail of corpses and forced labour in mines where black men cough and die and are so easily replaced ... I don't know ... God seems very patient with the pioneers of civilisation ...

## Thursday, April 8th, 1920

L ast night passed slowly ... The jail was full of little
noises, knocking in some far cell ... footsteps on the
gravel far down below the window ... the cautious tread of
warders on their rounds of peeping ... somebody clearing
his throat in a cell near by ...

As dawn came I dozed and shot awake again, forgetting
where I was until the triangle clanged in the circle. The
prison was being called out of that sleep which knows no
ideals, and no stout-barred windows as the price of them,
impersonal sleep which has no partisanship and takes no
sides ... The triangle boomed the jail back into wakefulness
and warders and warded ...

Half an hour later the passages ring with the loutish
sounds of banged-back bolts as every door is opened and
the slopman with his loathsome bucket pollutes the air in
every cell and goes his way unheeding. It is half-past six ...

At half-past eight the porridge ... that will not be eaten ... At ten the doctor, and after him the careful climb down the iron stairway to the ground floor, and thence to the exercise-ring and the kiss of the cold air ... At one o'clock the dinner that will go back as it came ... and at two we must do honour to the Governor by standing at our tables, though we do not honour him at all, or even like him ... Then the strong black cocoa that will cease to steam and grow thin as the grains fall, and at five the cell doors close, not to stir again until the agony of the slop-bucket begins another day ... Jail life is so queer.

At exercise Philip was more jubilant than ever ... He walked swiftly with panther steps ... 'Fifteen more came in last night,' he said, 'and they are all from Tipp ... Things are going A1 outside. Castle nervous as hell ...'

He left me to greet one of the Tipperary men: 'God bless us, Seán, and is it you?' ... It was ... I saw no more of him until we were going back to our cells ... I stumbled ... His hardness and his buoyancy both vanished, his arm was as gentle around me as a woman's ... 'Getting weak?' he asked, with wonderful softness in his voice.

'Not a bit of it,' I said. 'Kicked a raised flagstone' ... Getting weak ... h'm ...

# Friday, April 9th, 1920

The jail is almost full. Men from all parts ... Northmen and far Westerners and the liquid speech of Kerry ...

Twomey shares Philip's optimism today ... Not a man has broken strike ... The worst period is over ... Several carried to hospital last night after lock-up, but the strike is going on there as here. Tomorrow will decide ... It is certain now that some of the sick men will go out tomorrow ... And then the strike is won ... If any go, all go ... Friendly warder passed the word a few moments ago that the prison doctors are fighting hard for releases in the morning.

Never felt so happy ... Today we laughed a lot at one another's weakness in the ring, and found it best to remain sitting most of the time ... Philip says we must husband our strength to walk home in the morning ... Feel the jail gates giving way ... The joy of freedom, with victory added to it, is suffocating ... Was very tired and gloomy this afternoon.

Sleeplessness is so much harder to bear than fasting ... But tonight I feel that we have not suffered enough, that our victory has been too easy ... It seems unfair to have such a triumph for such little pain ... The first man that leaves tomorrow leads us all out ...

## Saturday, April 10th, 1920

Yes, that *is* the Angelus. That wisp of sunlight will soon have climbed from ridge of bolts to ridge of bolts up the black door, and then ... then it will be dark ... But nothing has happened. They said if we held out until Saturday we would have won; that men would go out on Saturday and that the rest would follow on Monday ... They said that ... But nobody has gone out, and Saturday has gone out ... They said they daren't let men die ... But men are dying ...

Why is nobody singing in his cell? ... Do they all think that ... that now it must be death ... and such a queer death? ... What a silence there is! Yet it seems a silence full of mad conflict ... the conflict of minds fighting out the struggle of life with death ... with death that will go on for days and days ... If only I had left unsaid that thing about Davin. It was so needless and bitter ... But why is nobody singing? ... That is so strange ... It is dark now ... Ah, that deep-voiced man below is singing, not loudly, but the prison is so still ... Curse that warder and his new boots ... Ah, I hear him again now ...

> So all round me hat I wear a tri-coloured ribbon O;
> All round me hat until death comes to me;
> And if anybody's askin' why I'm wearin' that ribbon O,
> Ye can tell them 'tis for love of him I never more shall see.

Oh! I wish he wouldn't ... If sleep would only come tonight ... If thoughts would only stay away ... They said there would be releases on Saturday ... What if there were never any releases? ...

'Ye can tell them 'tis for love of him I never more shall see.'

Yes, I suppose they will sing that ... I wonder where they will bury us? It will be funny, all the coffins ... I must have those books sent back to Ben ... If it were light I could read ... Christ, give me one hour's sleep ...

## SUNDAY, APRIL 11TH, 1920

What's that? The light fell fair into my eyes … It was the man on the hourly round with his lantern … At least he might take this night off …

'Hallo!'

'What d'ye want?'

'What's the time, please?"

'Two o'clock.'

'Oh! Lord.'

… And the rubbered feet moved up the ward, halting at every door. The prisoners around me and below me I heard stirring. The night had begun for all of us again … What a tragedy 'regulations' can become! …

Did you ever notice that the city clocks are all so pleasantly out of time that, as they strike the quarters and halves and hours, they take it up one after another like school-children singing a roundelay? After a little while you get to know this chime from that; and what the role of each is; and how he never misses it. You hear the domineering clocks on the big business houses trying to shout down the others. Yet, it is always the sweet-voiced clocks that, half-heard though they be, stay ringing in your mind ... There is a humanity in clocks ...

Perhaps they meant next Saturday ... Yes, I now see that answer to Philip. A man who is not always armed will arm himself when going on a 'job'; nor will he think himself a coward for it. Where, then, the cowardice in a man going to death arming his soul for its job? He will understand that. His philosophy gives him no way of escape. Glad I thought of that ...

I think I have been sleeping ... With the day, who cares? ... Hunger-striking is simple, after all ... Just fasting and no pain ... no pain ... But the heart stops. That is the trouble. They say men have fasted for many days ... but when they were dying they were free not to fast. We must be glad to die. I was ... yesterday. Now it seems hopeless ... What do they care about a death, the brutes! ...

... Yet it is for Ireland, for justice, for ... for those who have not yet been taken that they may not have to do this ... this horrible unnatural thing ... But these are words and they mean nothing ... We are beaten ... I was ready to die on Friday ... There was hope then. And now? ... Now, it is Sunday morning and we are caged in here, panting and weak! ... Pearse's death ... He had only a day to think of it ... It was a soldierly death ... It meant something ...

I suppose they will not know that we are dead until they open the cell doors in the morning. The doctors will have to make calculations in their little notebooks to find out the exact hour ... Aunt Margaret ... she will go mad ... No ... It will be deeper than that ...

Oh, God let the daylight come ... This is the octave of Your resurrection. You came from the tomb. Bring us from our tombs ... Tombs ... Yes, each cell is a tomb ... Mountjoy has become a family vault ... Ha! Ha! ... They can peer in and see us in them ... I suppose they will have a three-penny day for the poor ...

I think I am going mad ... Four nights without sleep ... Six days without food ... Sounds like the beginning of one of Chesterton's poems ...

> Four nights without sleep ...
> Six days without food ...
> Four aeons without mercy ...
> Six kopeks a pood ...

A nonsense rhyme ... Belloc at his best ... Six kopeks a pood ... That is the Russian touch, suggesting the madness of Bolshevism to the anti-Bolshevik and the materialism of Czarism to the anti-Czarist ... Six kopeks a pood, besides meaning nothing, might well be the cry of a Czarist Chancellor about a tax, or of a Soviet leader about cheap bread. It has as much in it as any other world-cry … What is a kopek? What is a pood? … I think a kopek is a coin and a pood a weight. I don't know. It does not matter much now, at any rate …

The clocks again, thank God! … One … Two … Three … Fo … Fo … Ah! I missed it … But there's the Rathmines Town Hall … How long after the chime it strikes! … Ah! … One … Two … Three … Fo … F … *Three* o'clock! … Oh, God … God, I will take all the suffering of a generation on me tomorrow if I may sleep now …

Perhaps by thinking of drowsy things … bees … sunlight … tall, soft grass … the brilliant white wings of a butterfly … the beautiful blue wings … a dragon-fly over a murmuring summer stream … the shadow of an oak tree … a strange blue lake getting darker and darker … as the twilight comes creeping over it … slowly … slowly … the trees on the steep wooded banks lose their trunks now … the woods are blurring, too … they are purple now … they have lost their outline … they are falling into the soft, darkening sky … they are only a shadow … a … shadow … softly … deepening … a shad … ow … a …

'HALT! WHO GOES THERE?'

'Friend'.

Ha! Ha! … Friend indeed of you, Guardian of Death … There is to be no sleep tonight … Well … I accept that now … Must try to remember more clearly the essential things … Men must die. That is obvious now. Why should any object to being the first? … It will be hard to be the first … But, the others … it would be hard for them, too … Anyway, God is good … that is about the only thing one is sure of; and yet being sure of that, one is sure of everything …

Strange how the despair has passed entirely from me … There may be a meaning in that … Perhaps? … perhaps? … but no, not on Sundays … they never do.

Wonder how the others are. What if some of them be already dead? Am I responsible? Men joined the strike voluntarily … But was there not duress in the circumstances? And I did much to create the circumstances. Perhaps Brennan and his kiddies, perhaps he is dead … or Coleman – he fainted the first day … The fright he gave me … walking round the ring and suddenly clawing wildly at the rails, and in a flash hanging limp like a wet cloth against them … Some of the fellows laughed until they saw the trickle of blood from his blue lips … It was real! … Two got sick where they stood … Others sat down … Nobody spoke while Coleman was being carried off in the hospital chair … That day it was Coleman … Next day it might be anyone ... Or maybe little McCann is dead. God ... listen, God, it is better that one of us be the first. If it be Your Most Holy Will that men must die, let it be those of us who can most easily be spared ... It is a little thing to ask ... Under the weight of two or three corpses ... short-weight corpses, ugh! ... even those awful gates might give way ... We counted that there might be this cost ...

Must have raved all night ... thought I was stronger than that. But this sleeplessness is so unbearable ... And then the passing of all those laughing hopes of yesterday; hopes even Philip and Twomey held, dour men thought they be ... And I was worn out when I came in ...

But there must be no more mental panic after tonight. It is our business, us three at least, to keep our heads clear ... How glad I am that during it all the idea of compromise never came ... Compromise is impossible. Death we pledged ourselves to take instead, and will. But even half-sane to have remembered that, to have had it so clearly before me! ... that even an uncontrolled imagination darting in and out among dark thoughts, searching the closets of the mind, tearing up the very floorboards of the soul, could not find the idea of compromise – that gives me great strength ... My weakness is physical, nervous only ... I can still honourable hold my seat on the triumvirate ...

Rubber boots again …

'Hallo!'

'Yes.'

'What's the time?'

'Four o'clock.'

'Thanks.'

… I don't care now …

How quiet everything is … and dark … I might be already in my coffin … Perhaps I am … Perhaps … Oh! God … No, I cannot feel the sides of it … I would surely feel the sides of it … There is no coffin … But it is queer … there is no noise … no noise at all …

Be careful; be careful, the panic must not come again … Ah! it is half-past four … The porridge is a-making. I smell it. It fills the whole prison. They are preparing our breakfasts, which they know we shall not eat. Day after day these cans of porridge go back cold. Day after day new ones come, hot, steaming, the most enticing food in creation. People are starving within a hundred yards of this prison. They may starve! There will be less of them to send in here. We must not starve. That would defeat justice. If we die, they will shrug their shoulders and say 'suicide'. But when these others die they put us in here for saying 'murder'.

What a delicious smell it has! It seems hardly fair to the others to breathe it. Nice calculation how much nourishment there is in that smell. There must be some ... How keen the senses become with this fasting! Water has a thousand wonderful tastes. It is like drinkable moonstone in which each of these faintest, flickering colours becomes a taste so delicate that it is not even to be remembered a minute. Adam's Ale has a new meaning for me now, full of delicious depths ... So, too, with smoking. There is the fragrance of divinity in it. Everything in Virginia is there woven in and out among the little yellow threads of tobacco ... flowers and fruit and honey ... sunshine and far hazy meadows ... blue evening skies and the laughter of open-air children ... The curling smoke contains them all, the breath of them, the soul of them. The doctors say we must not smoke ... It depresses the heart, they say ... Not by medicine alone is man kept alive!

There, the prison day has started. They are beating the triangle ... What a jarring noise it is! But any noise is better than the silence ... I suppose the clanging has wakened all our men ... If any of them were asleep ... ha! ha!

I hear the criminals getting up ... The joy they must have looking forward to breakfast and work and the open air; to feel that they can walk, that they can live, that they need not die squalidly like this ... It is good to be a criminal in Ireland ...

'Are you for Chapel?'

'Yes, Warder.'

I got up. The weakness is not very marked yet ... gusts of faintness which soon sweep over, leaving me cold and trembling ... If there were only heat in the cells, perhaps fasting would not change us so quickly ... But 'regulations' say the heating of cells must cease on March 31st ...

... The church with its tawdry colours is almost empty. The warders are seated on those raised chairs which, at a crowded Mass, make them look like the mounted captains of a fleeing army ... Nine men and myself ... Ten out of almost a hundred left with strength to shuffle half a hundred yards ... The priest is saying Mass softly and quickly ... The warders are expectant ... They are thinking we shall suddenly lose the little strength we have ... ... Hallo! ... A settlement? ... Surely no? ... They would have called me ... Yet the men are cheering in their cells, are beating their doors, are calling one to another through the broken lamp-holes, are laughing! ... It must be very good news ... The order for release! ... It is wonderful to hear of it here: here before the altar, just when the Host has been elevated and the Divine Blood lifted up ... Assuredly our cause is just when it ends at such a moment ...

... But it is only half-past eight ... How could word come so early? Officialism always observes the Sabbath. The only Commandment it ever keeps ... But the men must be cheering for something, and for something wonderful … Even Fr McMahon thinks so … he is hurrying; the rippling music of his Latin has become a drone … His outspread hands are shaking …

There at last … ' … and of the Holy Ghost, Amen.' … How long they take to unkey that door … Hurry, Warder; can't you hear the men cheering? But prison kills the imagination. 'Regulations' say it must take so long to open a door … There it takes twice as long … The warders don't seem even interested … Perhaps 'regulations' say they must not hear prisoners howling and roaring like these outside …

… No, not releases … The prison passages are dotted with ugly heaps of porridge humped up in little lakes of blue-white mild … One has to step warily … A week ago men were told to break the glass lamp-holes in the cell doors … cautiously, six tonight and six tomorrow night, lest the simultaneous breaking result in handcuffs and strait-jackets, which made the strike last October so hard. Through this hole they were ordered to spoon the food if it were forced into the cells, to spoon it out over the passages … As we came along and found a heap missing we called to the delinquent to get up and spoon it out … We heard milk splashing behind us … They can clean up the prison with the satisfaction of knowing that temptation, to be effective, must be individual …

Heard Philip say to the Deputy who had followed us out from Mass: 'Verling, you cur, was it you gave that cowardly order?' ... The Deputy hurried past.

'Oh! My God,' he gasped, looking down the passages. To a warder who could hardly hide his smile he half-called, half-whispered: 'Take it out; take it out before these others get back.' 'These others' were we who were wading back from Mass ... Would hazard the prophecy that there will be no more food forced into the cells ...

Philip, as it turned out, should have been grateful to the Deputy for what he did. The men's determination to go on has become savage ... The gloom that had settled upon all our souls since the ringing of last evening's Angelus has melted away under the hot joy of spooning clammy porridge out through a small hole in an iron door ... The singing has begun again ... It is a landing flowing with milk and porridge! ...

Late in the afternoon the Governor came into the cell with a long manilla envelope in his hand. On it were written seven names. He explained, with no self-conviction in his voice, that it was an offer of settlement which he hoped would ...

'Read it,' I said.

Ha! Ha! ... An offer! ... Seven of us are to be deported if we are good boys and fatten up for it ... Not a word about the others … No offer of prisoner-of-war treatment for them.

None even for the seven, who through the benevolence of the British Government are to be imprisoned in England, without trial; instead of being imprisoned, without trial, in Ireland … Of course, the bait is that the seven to be deported will probably get political treatment in England … So it turns itself into a bribe to seven of us to desert the others … What I said to the Governor was not charitable … I like him for not answering …

Drafted a strong reply rejecting the offer as insulting. Philip and Twomey agreed with the draft. Together we toured the cells to read our answer to the men …

Ghastly pilgrimage … Some of the men almost unconscious. Nearly all horribly worn out … Did not guess it had gone so far … Harry, in reply to my remark that now these offers had begun others would soon follow, said almost inaudibly: 'If I am to hear any others, they had better hurry.' Some just looked at us curiously. As we explained and read, the curiosity left them. When we had finished they merely closed their eyes, and we tip-toed silently out. Such an offer after seven days of horror merely confirmed for them the things they had thought when the cell was dark … Two or three men, as they saw us enter their cells, lifted themselves in their beds with faces lit up with hope

… They soon fell back again, one drawing the blanket over his head to hide the look we had already seen … Three men were an ashen blue from the cold. Two of them, after the first few sentences, looked at us vaguely, without understanding, as calves do, and were silent … One talked to us about his mother as we read … another giggled vacantly … If it should go many more days some of these men will for ever be beyond offers, or, at least, beyond the possibility of ever again understanding them. Aiden, who is seventeen, and Gay, seventeen-and-a-half, showed excited approval of the strength of the reply: 'That's the stuff to give them!' sitting up in the bed to put more force into the declaration. Others approved also, more quietly. These were older men. Barney suggested a change which we made … Twomey, as we left the last cell, stumbled and fell … Philip and I tried to smile at one another after we had got him back to bed … No, we shall go on no more pilgrimages …

Read the reply for the Governor. He listened, slightly bowed towards us, eyeing us expectantly at first, then wistfully … quaint little man … We urged on him the necessity for speed …

'The men are dying,' Philip said simply.

The Governor asked us if we would take anything while we were waiting for the answer.

'How anything?' I asked.

46

'You must be very tired,' he said. 'I thought a warm drink …'

Strange how they will never, never understand.

'We will take something,' said Twomey, 'when we are given what we ask for in that.'

The Governor hurried away …

The three of us were sitting in Twomey's cell when I heard my name called outside …

'Visiting Justice to see you,' said Warder Smith, putting in his head.

'Tell the Visiting Justice we do not see enemy officials.'

A pause … Whispering outside … Warder Smith again:

'Mr Cahill would like to see you.'

Went to Mr Cahill, who had thus divested himself of alien honours. He proved to be one of those men who cannot say anything without making a speech. Evidently one of the rewards of a long and honourable life on public boards! I held on to the wire-caging, waiting for him to come to the point. Then I said:

'But, Mr Cahill, what have you *done*?'

Told me he had resigned, adding: 'There will be a great sensation in the morning.'

Simple Mr Cahill … We resigned, sixty of us, a week ago; twenty-two later arrivals had resigned since … The job we had thrown up in protest was the permanent one of being alive ... And there was no 'sensation in the morning.' Nor does it look now that there will be any until our resignations are accepted ... Ugh!

All I saw in Mr Cahill's story was that he had forced French to pledge himself to 'no concessions' ... Did not tell him that ... He had done his best ... So I thanked him instead ... He made a long, long speech to me ... It was cold standing there in the passage ... There are better things than living to be an old and valued member of half a dozen public councils.

French's reply brings it nearer home that there will have to be deaths ... Unless, in the end, the Press campaign Erskine has go under weigh will overwhelm him ... Need not tell this to the others ... They will learn soon enough ... They took a week to offer seven of us deportation ... The sum in proportion means a fast of nearly three months ... And if it takes three months' hunger-striking to get us all deported ... how long will it take to get us all released? ... Ha! ha! They won't be able to see us to release us then ... Meanwhile 'the law must take its course.'

Have seen the Sunday papers ... There were crowds outside the prison last night, praying ... Their hope seems also to be gone ... They have fallen back upon faith ...

No sunset tonight ... Last night just before the sun died it painted a poppy-field on the white wall immediately over the door ... It had achieved the perfect and, as man should, then passed out of the world ... Tonight it is raining ... How beautiful if a rainbow were reflected into the cell! ...

Hear singing and cheering outside ... The children's shrill voices are getting on my nerves ... Am I in for it again tonight? ... Had hoped today's excitement ... the long, horrible tour of the cells, would have tired me out and made me sleepy ... The cell is dark already ... If I could make out a programme, an itinerary for wandering thought. The names of all the people I know? ... God, no! That would be to create the desolation I must not feel tonight if I am to be the same tomorrow ...

A poem? ... Yes, I'll compose a poem ... Cannot those people with the shrill voices go away? ...

That lunatic of a cattle-driver is calling again through his cell window for cheers for the Republic. He has been at it all the evening ... What a voice he has! ... On a dark night he might have been driven himself ... Easy to know he has not been hunger-striking ... There he is: 'Hip-pip!' ... Nothing doing, my dear man ... 'Hip-pip!' ... There they are; our fellows think it is up to them to cheer ... Heavens, what a pathetic noise! ... 'Hip-pip!' ... About twenty of them cheering from the floors of their cells ... This is gruesome ... Must stop that fool ...

'Hallo!'

49

'Hallo!'

'Is it you're hip-pip-ing?'

'What?'

'Are-you-the-man-calling-for-cheers-for-the Republic?'

'Yes.' (Proudly) 'Hip-pip!'

'H-a-l-l-o!'

'Yes?'

'Would you mind going to bed and staying there. If you have nothing else to do for the Republic, remember we would prefer to die for it after a little sleep.'

That has quietened him ... Hope I haven't hurt him ... No, not a man with a voice like that ... Now for that poem ...

Hallo! ... What's up? ... Three warders running ... The doctor! ... The cell door they are opening is on this side ... Christ, as a brother, whoever it is, put Your arms about him now ... Oh, why, why, must it last as long as this? ... They are coming back slowly ... shuffling along ... I can just see out through the little hole ... That strange silvery light they have in prisons is almost worth coming in to see ... Their shadows! ... They are passing now ... carrying him ...

'Hallo!' (whispered).

'Yes.'

'Who is it?'

'Shanley.'

'Good heavens, he was splendid today. Is he bad?'

'Yes.'

'Go quietly … The men are very shaken, and this kind of thing will lead to others if they know.'

'Right.'

He has been taken to hospital … In the half-light I saw his head lolling as the chair swayed … Thrilled me horribly … Hospital must be pretty full by now … The shock has weakened me …

But that poem? … Oh! damn that poem! … Yet, no … I must employ my mind somehow if I am to use it again … And sleep … sleep has become a joke … That line I thought of yesterday …

## MONDAY, APRIL 12TH, 1920

I have been asleep ... ASLEEP! ... The poem did it ... At last my verse is justified ... Let me see:

> Let the wind, let the wind laughingly call,
> Swaying the trees with the rhythm of God,
> Tossing – great miser – the gold of the fall,
> Smoothing – great mother – the hair of the sod.
> Great is your charm, four great winds of the sky,
> Greater is hers ... hurry by.

Do not like 'the hair of the sod'; but the idea of the wind as a mother smoothing it, I like that ... It went on:

> Let the sun, let the sun slip through the day,
> Building gold roads through the unbuilded green,
> Steeping far hills in the blue of the bay ...

In the blue of the bay ... of the bay ... Oh! yes, I was held up there. Could not think of anything rhyming with 'green' that would do ... I must have fallen asleep turning over and

over these last three lines ... Wonder what the time is? ...
Hope it is nearly day; but I feel it is earlier than that ...
Must wait for the clocks ... But I have my watch! Refused
to give it up to the Deputy the night we came here. Forgot
that ... How far away it seems now ... What a truth was
in that phrase I flung at him that night: 'You'll be a sorrier
man that I came into this prison than I am.' ... His face
yesterday morning when Philip called him a cur! ... Yes ...
Many a true word is spoken in jail ...

Where are those matches? ... Ah! That light blinds me;
it stings like smoke in the eyes ... Well, well! a quarter to
one ... That poem was not so good as I dreamt it was ...
Cannot have been asleep for more than a few minutes ...
But ... the watch is stopped ... I remember now ...

For fear I should know how slowly the nights were passing, I did not wind it on Saturday ... Stupid ... However,
it seemed wise at the time, like a lot of stupid things. It is
the circumstances under which a thing is done that make
it wise or foolish ... Pity our minds could not live three or
four days in front of our acts ... If mine did, it would probably be buried by this ... Ha! ha! ... It would be useful,
though, for ordinary purposes ... Writing would become
almost insufferably accurate, all criticism being foreseen ...
Men would understand men better ... They would understand the consequences of their own acts better ... No, life

is more tolerable as it is ... And death too, perhaps ... It would take away all the sweetness of anticipation ... There would be none of those mistakes which make men great and life wonderful ...

The clocks ... Half-past something ... Ssh! ... somebody coming ... Hear the pad of rubber boots ... The man with the lantern ... On the upper landing ... He'll be here in a minute ... That's O'Neill shouting at him:

'What the hell are you shining that thing into our eyes for? Do you think we are going to climb out of the ventilators?'

A mumbled reply ... Here he comes ... 'Hallo!'

'Yes.'

'What's the time?'

'Two o'clock.'

Must have slept about half an hour ... It is quite a good poem ...

What a fight this has become! ... No matter how it goes now, their prison system is smashed ... If men die, it is smashed ... If men live on to political treatment or release, it is smashed ... At first I thought political treatment would be better ... Now I think it must be release. For if on any terms we remain passive in their jails, they will fill them up with thousands of us ... That will be in our favour up to a certain point. It will anger the people; it will make them feel their subjection; it will keep the adventurers out of the movement, who the moment it becomes safe will swarm into it and turn it into a new Board of Erin ... But there must come a time when thousands of arrests, with all that they mean, desolate homes, the breaking of the thrilling friendships of young men, lost positions, poverty, anxiety, hardships, loneliness – there must come a time when these things will tell upon the faith of the people and many will sigh for relief ... for any relief ... Yet history argues against that ... dead against it. In the bitterest periods of oppression Ireland lived more really, more ideally than in any of the periods of peace ...

Nations are so like men ... In poverty and desolation they remain faithful to their souls, who would lose them in luxury. It was only in peace-times that we became corrupt and forget or, worse, forwent our independence ... That is true ... But still, if we smash their prison system now, the men who, by reason of being here or in some other jail, are useless to the nation, can return to their Volunteering, to the constructive work of the Dáil, to the destructive work of many groups ... By smashing their prison system we become free to continue the smashing in Ireland of their Empire ... A few days' hunger in payment for such a blow is nothing ... Even a few deaths from hunger is nothing ... Again, this strike draws men's minds back to the origin of things … A hundred men are going to prove that an Irish Republic exists, exists visibly, actively; that the independence of Ireland was declared and is as much a fact as the independence of Belgium was in 1914 … When the replacement of Macpherson by Greenwood, of French by Macready, foreshadows 'negotiations,' it is well that the national belief in the existence of the Irish Republic should be announced to England and the world, aye, and to our own people, by a hundred dead bodies … Compromise will be impossible over our dead bodies …

What a destiny to be in Mountjoy with these issues gathered around one like friends, giving comfort and strength! … On us, though we did not foresee that, rests the fate of the people … If we fail, the nation fails … If we succeed, Ireland becomes more than ever 'the young girl with the walk of a queen' … Ireland! What is Ireland? … Land? … No. People? … No … Something else … I am not ready to die for earth or for a people … a people which is not very different from any other people … Ireland is something else … Ireland is the dead and the things the dead would have done … Ireland is the living and the things the living would die for … Ireland is the Spirit … It is the tradition of the laughing courage of men upon whose heads the pitch-cap has been placed by friends … It is the tradition of undefeat … of indomitable failure …

of love for an ideal as strong as the love of the Apostles for Christ as He quivered upon the Cross ... The crucifixion of Ireland is interminable and so her apostles are innumerable ... Ireland is justice, is truth ... That Ireland with that Christ-like spirit which God breathes into subject peoples ... *that* Ireland I am willing to die for; I wish, I long to die for ... Today or tomorrow this boasting may be tested ... I am not afraid, now ... When these, the essential things, are clear, death has none but a beautiful meaning ... But ... I would prefer to die in the daytime ... It is no harm to have a preference ... It would be so horrible at night ... There is the inevitable paradox in this: the weaker we become, the stronger we prove ourselves to be ...

I smell the porridge ... The night has passed quickly ... It will soon be daylight ...

Have seen the papers ... Lord French *has* pledged himself to no concessions ... It is now merely a question of how long we can last ... There was always the chance of their forgoing their prison rules in the hope that the people would have forgotten they had ever sworn to keep them ... But now the head of the English Executive in Ireland has taken a definite decision publicly, leaving no loophole for compromise. The prison rules will not be changed. The issue is knit there, at any rate. Either that word is kept and we die, or it is broken and Lord French goes. These are the alternatives. French would never do this unless he knew he had the Government in England behind him; he has possibly their written word ... Very well ... Without having the strength to pick up the gauntlet he has thrown, we shall fight him and those crouching behind him, blood-lustful ... They will eat, drink and be merry in their mansions and Viceregal Lodges ... We shall lie awake, starve and be mad in this evil-smelling hell-house ... But it is we who shall win ...

There will surely be trouble outside ... A great horror must be upon the people ... Their helplessness makes it worse. Their imagination is on fire and they see in through these walls a gruesomeness that may come eventually, but is not here yet. If it lasts much longer, a tragedy must occur outside as well as inside ... Here it will be the cold, damp passing away of men who are already a week buried ... no noise ... a cough, perhaps ... almost a secret death ... But outside ... outside there will be terror in it and dignity, there will be the anger of God in it ... yes, and of the devil. As we grow weaker, as we struggle for breath and clutch at the rags on these beds, the people will become tremendous in their strength ... They will laugh horrible laughter and with naked hands tear our bodies out of this ... A tragedy? ... There will be no tragedy outside ... it will be the noblest fury in our history ... There are men in Ireland today who count the cost very little. These men, as we die one by one, will make history ... Perhaps for the greatness of Ireland it were better we died. It may be that if we die now, thousands, who would have to die later if we failed, can live ... As in the famine days ... a revolution, the wilful giving of a few hundred lives, might have saved hundreds of thousands ... It is good for us to die ... I think so ... Thank God there is now no alternative ...

'Oh! quite well, Doctor, thanks; how are the others?' He has stopped smiling, the doctor. Why should *he* be afraid? The men are not afraid ... except a little at night when ... when the mind will not stay quiet ... But even Christ had that physical fear ... 'O Father, if it be possible, let this cup pass from Me,' and then 'Nevertheless, not as I will, but as Thou wilt.'

McCrane, the warder, has been here with letters. One from Mary, written yesterday:

I am listening to the church bells chiming as I write, and it seems that I am hearing them chime in England and in every Christian land. I think of you and your friends: I think how it would be if Christ were to come again now – another crucifixion and more terrible than the Jews gave Him. Then I think of these people praying and how it means nothing – and ... what can one say?

... We suffer greatly these days. I want you to know this – that we do not forget ... that it is a load upon our hearts ... Shall we see you again? There are no words we can say – none which can tell the meaning of these things to us.

Whatever may befall, however the gods have planned to make use of us after death, something remains, indestructible, immortal, which even the gods cannot destroy.

'We are suffering greatly these days' … Aye, more greatly than we are suffering. That is the real pain of hunger-striking … to know that those outside endure so much … that it is a load upon their hearts. They imagine ten times more agony than is here and, imagining, feel it … We are powerless to dispel these weird, misshapen fears … Christ, help those who are in woe for us; they need it so much more than we … 'Shall we see you again?' Not now, I think … But I shall not say that …

That queer man Brady has been into my cell and out of it like a whirlwind … How he got into the jail I cannot imagine … He talked with his chin out about the solidarity of labour and the omnipotence of the workers of the world. In one of his speeches he said all we had to do was to hold out … something would be bound to happen … Not something, friend, … everything …

'Hallo, Warder!'

'Yes?'

'How did Mr Brady get in; has he been arrested?'

'No, the hunger-strikers in danger of death are given visits.'

So Brady was a visit! A restful person to send to those

'in danger of death'! … So I have joined that group now … Hope my people will take the warning I sent them and not come until they get a wire from me personally. It is an old trick to wire for relatives in the hope that they will induce the men to take food. But we warned the men against that before the strike started … They know what to say … Your tricks will be of little avail this time, Mr Jailer … The men are pledged to the lives of one another and the honour of Ireland … And these things are greater than father and mother, than wife and sister … My father has been here with Rory. Chaffed them for having been caught by the Governor's telegram. Told them I had no intention of becoming really ill until next Monday week … We fired pleasantries at one another during the quarter of an hour for which the British Government, having summoned them from Cork, allowed them to speak to me … but they were pleasantries that had been steeping overnight in tears …

Saw the same suppressed agony in my father's eyes as I had seen two years ago … His son was dead, then … Rory, who was with him then, was with him now … What a double tragedy that journey must have been! … The six hours, during every minute of which the rhythm of the train sang the one thing he wished to forget … The telegram … the time of the year … the associations … the uncertainty … the overcrowding sorrow of that former journey … the overcrowding agony of this ... What a man he is! ... He shook my hand going away, giving it that slightest extra pressure which, interpreted, meant despair and pride ... and gave me happiness and strength and a strange, weird loneliness, all distinct, yet indistinguishable ... Then he turned hurriedly and went out. He could have looked back. He didn't. Rory did ... His eyes were happy eyes. He is as we are. He knows the fight must go on in dirt and wretchedness as well as in the fields ... Jim died in the field ... April 20th, 1918 ... What if that be my day too? ... This is the 12th ... I might last. But, if I did not sleep ... I hope God will not let me last if I do not sleep ... Eight more is the 12th ... I might last. But, if I did not sleep ... I hope God will not let me last if I do not sleep ... Eight more days ... How strange if I lived through them! ... how horrible if that be my day too! ...

No answer yet to the rejection we gave yesterday to the Governor's offer ... It is certain they have made up their minds to break us ... They will find it harder than they think ...

Denis and Owen and Rory came in this evening ... As we were chatting I saw a chance of escape ... Owen's or Denis' Roman collar and coat and ... freedom ... life ... They saw it as well as I. Owen got quite excited. Explained I could not go, yet ... If we had won or were certain of winning, it could be done ... But not now with the shadow of death upon us. If was all the men who had to be saved, not any one ... Said I would try if the strike ended with prisoner-of-war treatment ... We would be too weak at first to take visits downstairs and would get them like this, in the cells ... Ten minutes after they had gone I had planned everything out ... Half an hour later I had successfully escaped many times ... An hour – and the whole prison had passed out in newly-shaven faces and Roman collars and black coats ... When the strike is over and we are given visits in the cells, that will be the time for the clerical tailors! This strenuous mental prison-breaking has set me on fire ... Physically even, I feel I have run many miles. ... People would laugh if I told them I had a pain in my neck from looking back at my pursuers ...

That is Philip's voice ...

'Hallo, boys!'

I hear the men crawling to the doors of their cells to listen at the broken lamp-holes.

'Yes, Philip.'

'There is to be a General Strike tomorrow.'

The majority of the men are cheering lustily ... There are silent ones ... They feel that the General Strike has come too late ... I wonder ...

The evening paper is filled with news of us. The Labour

Manifesto calling for a General Strike sounds the right note:

> These men, for the greater part our fellow-workers and comrades in our Trade Unions, have been forcibly taken from their homes and imprisoned without charge ... in outrageous defiance of every canon of justice. They are suspected of loving Ireland and hating her oppressors – a heinous crime in the sight of tyrants, but one of which hundred's of thousands of Irish working men and women proudly acclaim their guilt ...
>
> Today, though they are on the point of death their titled jailers venomously shriek, 'Let them die.' We, workers, dare not allow this tragedy to come to pass ... As trade unionists we have only one weapon left – a general strike ...

I see, too, that the Dublin Corporation has unanimously endorsed the calling of the strike and has adjourned in protest ... Heavens, how great a thing this strike has grown into ... What a power there is in every individual if the gods are propitious and he himself will act as he advises! ... Two years ago the English prison system could have been smashed. It would have meant lives ... It is going to mean more lives now ... Had there been an Ashe tragedy every three months for a year there would have been none of this promiscuous raiding which now fills a prison in a night ... Derry, Belfast and Wormwood Scrubs should have been linked up with us from the first ... Thought of that on the second day of the strike ... Meant to send word out ...

Forgot about it in the novelty of fasting ... Word should be sent to them now to notify the respective Governors that at the first death here they take up the strike ... Shall suggest that to Philip.

Feel tonight that we have them beaten ... They will take life from us, of course ... partly because we have damaged the roots of their gallow-tree; partly because they will want to show that they are really strong ... But this General Strike and the publicly declared sympathy of public bodies all over Ireland make it certain that they will suffer defeat in the end ... And the more lives they take before they inevitably yield, the more profound will be their defeat ...

It is quite dark ... All day long the people outside have been cheering and singing ... Heard the hymn, 'Hail, Glorious St Patrick,' quite distinctly ... Thousands must have been singing it ... From a distance girls' voices sound much more beautiful than men's ... There is a spiritual exaltation upon the people ... Strange what life death gives ... It seems that only by tragedy the soul of a people may be saved ... From the beginning of this awakening, tragedy, or the shadow of it, has been the dominant *motif* ... The executions in 1916; Ashe's death in 1917; the solemn preparations in 1918 to fight conscription to the death; the sweeping into jail of all the leaders ... Dick Coleman's death in jail ... The General Election and the national tenseness for the militarist reply ... Pierce McCan's death in jail in 1919 ...

The beginning of the Military Terror ... The attempt to kill Lord French ... The sack of Thurles last January ... Curfew and military law ... The murder of the Lord Mayor of Cork ... the shock of it and the silent oath of vengeance of a nation ... Men and women shot down in Dublin streets barely three weeks ago ... The shadow of an Amritsar upon the faces of the people ... Volunteers stealthily oiling their rifles, counting their ammunition, stopping now and then to hold their breath and listen ...

Then, crowding on top of one another ... Alan Bell by the roadside at midday in Dublin ... James MacCarthy in his home at midnight in Thurles ... Thos. Dwyer in his sisters arms at the Ragg ... Easter Saturday morning with its military cordons: Easter Saturday evening with its blazing tax-collectors' offices and two hundred constabulary barracks ... And then this ... At first the adventure of a few men ... Now the greatest drama of a generation ... The players bloodless, moist, with the smell of death in them ... An audience of white, pain-lined faces, hungry for consolation ... A hushed, softly breathing people ... The singing of hymns against machine-guns ... Children calling for children, shrilly ... The coarse, sudden bulk of a tank ... The beautiful, delicate light of a match upon the bayonet of a soldier preparing to smoke ... Angry words near the tin-hatted cordon ... A blow ... The surge forward of thousands, snarling ... A bearded, habited priest with uplifted hand ... A fall of voices, then silence ... 'Hail, Mary! full of grace ...' The feverish, thunderous knocking of an aeroplane flying low ... 'Holy Mary, Mother of God ...' The warning shout of a sentry ... Mothers and fathers who entered the prison with the fire of resolution in their eyes, leaving it with a woe in them which not even the cordon of troops can make them hide ... They had not cried before their boys ... Who would stop them now? ... The respectful withdrawing of the crowd as they come ... The whispered sympathy ... The urgent questioning of children ...

What a play it is! ... Not the only actors now, these tight-skinned, clammy bodies on the prison pallets ... The whole Nation has crowded into the cast ... It is the world which has become the audience ... What music could be set to this by a master? ... beautiful music with a wail in it which would drive men mad ...

## Tuesday, April 13th, 1920

Men are nearly mad now ... Some of the other men ... I know ... But I am not mad ... They are trying to make me mad ... They are sending men to watch me for fear I should sleep ... Telling the sentries to shout when I seem like sleeping ... I heard them whispering it to the soldiers ... They went down to the end of the prison-grounds to whisper it ... They thought I couldn't hear them ... I can hear anything ... It doesn't matter how far away they go, I can hear them ... They are tramping past my door now because they think I am going to sleep ...

It is dark, but I see they are watching me ... I know they are ... If I were mad, I wouldn't know ... They are watching me ... They have red eyes like coals ... They think I don't see ... Ha! ha! ... Don't they know yet that Sinn Féiners see everything? ... They are waiting until I sleep, so that then they can steal in and take my mug of water away

… I would become mad more quickly if I had no water … They know that … Beautiful water with a thousand tastes … Perhaps if it had no taste they would leave it to me … If I could hide the mug, they might forget … But justice never forgets … Ha! Ha! … The Law must take its course … and my mug of water …

I shall fight then when they come … There are hundreds of them I don't care … They are gathering at the door to dash in and steal it … I can see them … Jesus love, give me strength now to fight them … If I have faith, I can be as strong as they … They think it is too dark for me to see … It is never too dark for me … And they forget that they have eyes like coals … red eyes like red coals … If they closed their eyes, perhaps I couldn't see them … But they couldn't see then … They will have to keep their red eyes open … fierce red eyes fixed on my soul, burning it … They are waiting to see fear in my soul … They will never see it … It is not of them I am afraid … I shall look at them too … I shall die looking at them … When I am dead I shall look at them … for ever …

Ah! they are afraid to come in … I have won … the red coals are dying out … I have torn them with my eyes … They are going away … They would steal my mug of beautiful water, little mug of water, … if they had the courage … They have no courage … They are going away …

making no noise ... stealing away ... ashamed, I suppose ... They know now that I am not mad ... They have gone away to wait ... to wait like tigers ... with nothing alive but their eyes ... their red eyes ... to wait until I am ...

I am perspiring ... Curious delusion that was ... It *has* made me weak ... Warders with red eyes ... Ha! Ha! ... Where did I get that? ... Wanting to steal my mug of water ... I can feel the itch of perspiration on my cheeks ... The delirium swept over me suddenly ... possessing me ... all of me ... What made me think they had red eyes? ... Ah! Yes ... The door opposite ... red, of course ... In the half-light I can see it through the lamp-hole clearly enough.

I must fight these mad thoughts when they come, the moment they come ... Otherwise they will eventually crowd in and stay in ... and ... ugh! ... better not think of that ... It will come if we have much longer to lie here, awake ... But it has not come yet ... Meanwhile I shall drink the health of those warders with the red eyes ... which, when I am sane, are sometimes such kindly eyes ...

Thought I put the mug here ... No ... Surely? ... I cannot find it ... So ... it ... was ... *not* ... madness! It was real, it was real; oh! my God, it was real. They *have* stolen it ... The cowardly brutes, they *have* stolen it. The mug of water, sweet mug of sweet water, kindly mug of water by

70

which I was living ... I suppose I fell asleep for a moment while I was staring at them ... When I thought I saw them going away, it must have been the blurring of drowsiness that was on me ... How quick they were! ...

But I heard no clanging of bolts ... That is strange ... I would have remembered that ... It would have wakened me ... I must have been asleep a long time, long enough to give them time to slip back the bolt noiselessly and with muffled keys to open the door ...

But what in Heaven's name would they want with my mug of water? ... The whole thing is ridiculous ... A match ... The light will pierce my eyes ... But I must know whether I am sane or mad ... They have no reason to take my mug away ... They are kind ... nearly all ...

There it is ... at the foot of the door ... books and clothes and newspapers huddled round it like a drunken guard ... Must have got up to hide it ... What possessed me to put it there? ... Yes, I suppose so ... They could not see it from outside, and if they opened the door to find it they would spill the water and not have the satisfaction of carrying it away ... Curious that I have no memory of getting up ... This is the price we have to pay to smash their prison system ... Seems a little like profiteering ...

I suppose those opposed to us do really believe that we are suicides ... If they cannot understand nationality, they cannot understand what we are doing or why we are doing it ... They speak of it as needless self-inflicted suffering ... Heigh-ho! but the whole thing is a riddle ... I know, in my own small circle, a dozen people who would go to death with us if they understood us; who see truly in every other way but this, and in this oppose us and would think it right to kill us ... Truly, 'Human nature's the divvil altogether.' ...

The porridge is a-making ... Another night has passed ... almost. Soon it will be day ... There will be visits ... Then evening and the distant whispering of thousands as they wait, wait for any word, any word at all but this ... this mad silence ... Then the light will die out of the cell; death will bring his shroud in ... it will be dark ... For years we shall wait for the day, and it will come at last. In God's mercy it always does come at last ... Then another day ... another night ... and ...

But it cannot go farther than that ... Wonder what these last few moments will be like? ... There will be terror in them, of course; the unknown is always terrible ... But there may be joy too ... There *will* be joy too: for with death the strike is won and a great battle is won ... By dying we drag down their prison system ... It will be buried in the great grave they are, perhaps, already preparing for us ... Their architects are even now sending in their designs and the builders are wondering how they can underpay the labourers who will dig and dig and curse us if the day is hot ... Our grave-clothes will be the hoods of their raiding lorries ... The lorries which, as the people scurry before Curfew, steal through the dark streets, marking the houses of the dead, rounding up men like cattle, putting wistfulness into the eyes of children ... These lorries, their unfleshed bones also showing, will be stored when we are stored ... Only *they* may be taken out again and used ... And we, we shall be taken out on the Day of Judgment, and probably we shall be glad to meet those who brought us in here, meet them on the Right Hand, too, only a little higher up ... It would very well happen ...

But by dying we win ... Of all things, that is certain ... Yet we shall not all die ... Three or four, perhaps ... They would like us all to die on the one night ... late at night, so that during Curfew they could creep into the street with us and bury us ... Maybe that is the origin of Curfew ... but, no: tyrants have little foresight ... One death today and two tomorrow and three the day after ... They will break under that strain sooner then we shall ...

The triangle ... It is six o'clock ... They are opening the criminal's doors ... Asked Warder McCrane last night to tell me first thing how the others are ... Hope he will remember ... But for the friendly warders this strike might have been already broken ... If they had tempted the men, some might have failed; and if any had failed, many would die, because the failure of the few would encourage the British to test every man to the uttermost ... The warders tempted the men in the other strikes ... But today they have been leavened with the mass of the people and it is no longer hard to make them understand ...

'Well, McCrane?'

'Brennan and Darcy are very bad. Brennan is going, I think. Some of the others are weaker. O'Connell has those fainting fits again. Rogers vomited half the night and is like a ghost.'

'Thanks, McCrane. By the way, what do you think's going to happen?'

'I don't know; some of you are going to be let die, sure enough.'

'We are ready for that, McCrane.'

'Yes, but it will be hard on us if some of you die. The people will not understand.'

'Well, McCrane, we have all to take our risks. It will be unpleasant for you; but it will be still more unpleasant for us. Cheer up, man. We may win yet.'

'Ye are great men.'

I wonder are we ... It seems a greatness thrust upon us ... Saw him looking at that yellow tin on the shelf ...

There is bread and margarine in that since the day before the strike ... Nine days now ... Once or twice I wanted it, yearned for it, desired it with every fibre in my body; just for a second each time ... Then its attraction ceased; when the mind is made up it is easy ... Noticed in yesterday's papers that some French journalist spoke of our 'pangs of hunger' ... Nobody would ever believe that there are none ... There is revulsion at death, a wild longing to live ... but no physical call for food ... that ceased on the second day ... Now tastes and smells are pleasant to think of, but mean nothing ... If the mind took the fast as quietly as the body does, the whole thing would seem like a joke, there would be so little suffering in it ... If our friends outside would believe this ... But it is true, and they never will ...

Two doctors this morning ... Dr Hurley's smile has completely worn off. He looks quite changed ... aged ... Sat on my table after Dr McConnell had gone out ...

'Now, Gallagher,' he said, 'I want you to get your brain working. No man has died yet. Some of them cannot live much longer. Brennan is nearly gone. Two of the men in hospital are dying. Some of the later arrivals in A. Wing are likely to go under any minute. I have got this thing through up to now without a death.' (I smiled with my eyes only: he is too kindly a man to hurt.) 'Cannot you think of some settlement?'

'Yes, Doctor: release.'

'They won't grant that, and you know it.'

'Prisoner-of-war treatment, then.'

'I am afraid they have really made up their minds not to give that either. Is there to be no give and take in this matter?'

'None, Doctor. We have tabled our demands and, with the help of God, we'll stick to them. They are just.'

'Well, I cannot keep the men alive for more than another day unless they take something. Stimulants or something.'

'They will take nothing, Doctor.'

He went out without saying a word … Poor man! he seems to be suffering more from the strike than we are.

Have just been given a letter from Brennan by Warder O'Kelly. Horrible letter … Brennan says he has fasted nine days … It is not his courage which is lacking. But he has seven kiddies … If he dies, they starve … 'My heart is torn out of me thinking of them,' the letter says. 'The Doctor told me this morning that I cannot live without brandy. I would not ask it for myself … If you say no, I will not take anything' … My first impulse was to let him decide for himself whether he should take anything or not … Then realised that, horrible though refusal was, this was the rest case … The answer, if other men's lives are to be saved must be, 'Take nothing.' … A bitter answer … Yet, how can it be otherwise? ... If this strike breaks, not ourselves alone, but Ireland is beaten ... Men must die ... But it is awful to have to kill men ... to have to starve little children ...

Oh! I wish it had never begun ... And it was I ... I who began it! ... For what? ... Aye, for what? ... Ireland? ... nonsense! ... Justice? ... piffle! ... For vanity; that was it, for vanity! I wanted to show how strong I was ... What a great fellow I was ... I had been saying outside that I would never again remain in prison for more than a fortnight ... They would have said I was a boaster if I had remained ... And so I did this thing ... Dyer murdered hundreds of innocent men that he might not be laughed at ... Where is the difference? ...

Surely this isn't true ... But if it isn't, why did I thrust these thoughts away yesterday and the day before? ... I am afraid of them ... If they were not true, why should I be afraid of them? ... So that is it ... vanity ... cowardice before people I do not even care about ... That it what Brennan must die for and his children, little children, starve for ... It is too late to stop it now ... The others are dying for Ireland ... They will not know that I am dying for vanity ... But ... I will know ... The thought of it will never leave me now ... I had not seen it so clearly before ... At least I shall pay for my vanity ... It will cure me of it ... I shall never be vain again ... I shall never have a chance to be ...

Fr O'Carney has been here. Came into the cell, serious-eyed.

'I am sorry,' he said, 'that they have started this General Strike.'

'Won't it succeed, Father?'

'It isn't that; they should have delayed it; the strike might have been settled today without it.'

'How?' I said, sitting up.

'Well, the Chaplain and I had written a very strong letter to the Prisons Board, very strong indeed. They could hardly have continued their attitude in face of it.'

'Oh!' I said, lying down again.

Everybody seems to have become very simple.

Then he drew over the table and sat on it, looking at me, querulously. I anticipated much of what he had to say; but I listened quietly as he went step by step towards disclosing what his face disclosed when, in preparation for his carefully worded little speech, he put his hand behind him to feel for the table to sit upon.

He wondered whether he could make a suggestion ... entirely unofficial, I would understand ... Would we state some terms of settlement which he, if he should accidentally see the Under-Secretary ... (a little bow as 'accidentally' was spoken) ... might mention to him as acceptable? ... Could he propose anything to James (he called him James) which he could say that he believed ... (another little bow at 'believed') ... the strikers would consider reasonable? ... He would not do it in an official way, 'of course.' ... He would just mention the terms to James as terms it 'might' ... (third little bow at 'might') ... be worth offering ... He would say nothing about seeing us, 'of course.' ... Was there nothing which in that way he could propose? ...

I said certainly ... He could propose prisoner-of-war treatment or release ... Then thought it better to see Philip and Twomey. Philip took the wiser attitude. No 'backstairs' negotiations. No recognition of the existence of James. Went back to Fr O'Carney ... Told him we knew nothing of James except that he was in the pay of our enemies. Was glad to get that shaft in ...

On the third day of the strike Fr O'Carney had come into the cell and scolded me and all the others for committing suicide. Said he would have to refuse men Absolution after the ninth day as they would then be face to face with death, and continuance of hunger-striking would become an intention to take their own lives. Pointed out the poverty of the unnamed authorities he quoted: 'Some of the best theologians in Ireland,' he called them ... I suggested that the Catholic Church was older than Christian Ireland or its very modern theologians; that it was universal, not insular. I demanded an authoritative interpretation of the Fathers.

When his temper cooled, I suggested that his mind was predisposed to considering the hunger-strike suicide, and that his moral standards were affected, if even slightly, by his political views. 'You hold, Father,' I said, 'that revolution is unjustifiable.' 'Revolution,' he answered, 'is never justifiable.' I saw he would never understand our position, so we spoke of the glare of white-washed walls and the effects of smoking on the nerves.

I had to think it all out when he had gone away. The issues he had raised, although subconsciously I felt them to be false, were tremendous issues, reaching out into eternity, reaching in into the very centre of the soul. There were momentous political issues as well. If the men were refused Absolution, the strike might collapse. It was the only thing that could break us. That was on the third day. On the ninth this greatest of crises would come. The ninth was distant then. But with the shutting up of the prison on Saturday the spiritual unrest became almost unbearable. By yesterday I had unravelled most of the doubts … and now I just fight each fear as it comes, stifling it more than dispelling it … The price for the calm that eventually came to me was nearly too great to be paid. Even now the thing stands as a shadow within me, darker far than the shadow of death … I can but trust in the great common sense of God.

The discussion I mentioned to none. I could not without

putting into another soul the anguish in mine ... So night after night I met the procession of dread alone and bent my head until it passed ... The ninth day I felt would be a black day for us all. When it dawned this morning I half-laughed at all my fears ... But it was a small recompense ...

Today when I saw Fr O'Carney again, and remembered his royally-minted philosophy, I had little kindness in my heart for him. I recalled, too, that he had said it was he who 'settled' the Christmas strike ... There was anger in his eyes as he left me ... There was a greater in mine ...

Later, the Governor came in alone ... He looked drawn and white and despairing ... I pitied the little man: he has to fight a fight which he hates, using weapons which terrify only himself ... He seemed anxious to discuss things ... I encouraged him ... He began by saying matters had gone so far we should try to come to some agreement ...

'Why do you do this thing?' he asked. 'When you smash the prison, cells, everything, we know what to do: you remember when you were here last? But this hunger-striking makes it so difficult for us.'

'That is why we hunger-strike,' I said; 'we can always beat you by hunger-strike: if not by release, then by death.'

'But is there no way out: nothing you can think of?'

'Oh! yes,' I said; 'release.'

'Ah!' he said, 'I cannot grant that.'

'Prisoner-of-war treatment, then, Governor.'

'But that, if it is ever to be granted, will take days to decide upon.'

'The only other alternative is death,' I said.

'Is there nothing immediate that would save these men from dying? The doctors say there is little chance of keeping some of them alive after tonight.'

'Nothing, Governor.'

He stood looking down at me with open despair in his face. Then he went out ... The Doctor, the Under-Secretary, the Governor, all looking for a settlement ... The first good sign ... The officials are beaten ... But those above them ... they will not yield so easily ...

The Governor was back in my cell two hours later ... a little triumphant ... He had just received a new offer ... Twenty men to be deported and, while awaiting deportation, to be given 'ameliorative treatment.'

'Well?' he said when I did not reply.

Tell whoever sent that, that if he thinks he can bribe twenty of us to desert the others he will have to think again. No settlement which does not include all will be listened to.'

He went out, dropping his gloves as he went.

Drafted a reply to this new offer, and when Philip and Twomey, to whom the Governor had also gone, came up

I submitted it … It was very strong … Strength we must have now above everything. Their line has broken … They have, despite His Excellency's telegram, offered 'ameliorative treatment.' … Those on top are also being beaten … If only we had a few days more to fight them to their knees and live! … Philip and Twomey agreed with the draft and we presented it to the Governor … We made no pilgrimage with it … The days of pilgrimages are over … except the great one … When the Governor had gone, Philip said he just had word from G.H.Q. that the Castle and the British Cabinet were determined to let some of us die. Felt suddenly cold as Philip spoke … My head throbbed a little … The gleam of hope vanished … G.H.Q. are not often wrong …

I was going on strike … Forget most of what he said … It was so little interesting in comparison with his face … No humour in his face … Almost no light in it … Hard thin lips, hard piercing eyes, good features with no softness anywhere in them … We had not met before, but his face had his history upon it. He is the type of the men who count the cost very little … There would probably be light in his face in battle, especially if he were cornered and one bad aim meant death to him … I can see him laughing then … He laughed seldom and as he looked, hardly … His type is the Irish militarist … When I met him I realised I would never be a real soldier ... In these days I shall try to do what a soldier does ... I shall advise all young men in Ireland to do as soldiers do ... But I shall advise none to become soldiers ... Ireland needs many men like Philip; but it is Ireland's tragedy to need them ... Men without softness anywhere in their faces are found in subject peoples, creating revolution. But in Empires they are found – creating Amritsars ...

During discussion on this latest offer, Philip, who was sitting on the foot of my mattress, had the patch of window-light full on his face. I studied it and its few expressions. When he announced that G.H.Q. had given up hope, I think he nearly smiled ... Such a man likes to be hopeless, so free a hand does it give him. Glanced for a moment at Twomey ... Twomey is malleable ... If it comes to a difference between Philip and myself, Twomey will side with Philip, because Philip is stronger than I ...

Owen and Denis have been in again ... There are thousands waiting outside ... Their anger is growing ... God help us if it breaks before its time ... There are tanks, machine-guns, rifles ready for it if it break before its time ... G.H.Q. are right ... They have ringed the prison round with barbed wire and are waiting until the first death turns the praying into howling ... Then after a little time there will be many silent. They have trebled the cordons ... 'And they ... made the sepulchre sure, sealing the stone, and setting guards.'

... They are afraid that the people may get sudden strength and, coming by night, steal our bodies ... How horrible the subjection of a people! ... But the people are stronger than they ... The line of unarmed Volunteers who are standing between the people and the troops, these are stronger than all their men and all their armament ... I can hear the people gibing the Tommies in their war-kit ... I can almost see them falling back before the Volunteers in their shoddy ... I wonder are Ernie and Farrell somewhere in that Volunteer cordon ... They will mind ... I suppose they are thinking of that night ... and the laughter when the danger was over ... It is painful to remember laughter ...

It is getting dark ... The sentries are calling halt more frequently and louder ... They are nervous ... They have posted double sentries ... Perhaps they fear a rescue ...

A rescue ... rescue ... Heavens, if it were possible! ... Why shouldn't it be? ... If it is possible, it will be done ... G.H.Q. have lost hope ... Men who have lost hope gain daring ... A hundred will die if they do not move ... Far less than a hundred will fall in a carefully planned rescue ... Had I only thought of this before ... I could have sent out a plan ... But Carroll and Flynn were here not so long ago. They will be thinking hard tonight ...

... What if, when the night is very black and silent, I should hear men stealing in stockinged feet, a sound only a man waiting for death could hear ... Then suddenly the steps would cease ... There would be the slightest grinding on the gravel and the gasp of a sentry as he went down ... The creak of the gate to the excercise-ring ... A terrible silence as everybody waited to find out if it had been heard ... A long silence, taking away the power to breathe ... Then running feet in the passages ... The cautious opening of cell doors ... Names whispered joyfully ... The shadows of many men passing and re-passing in the ghostly light of the prison ... A strange rabble trooping out ... Some carried ... Ropes and ladders and cars ... Laughter and love and sleep ... Oh! if it could be done ... If it can be, it will ... The letting in of relatives gives the chance for some to come in and help from inside ... It may not be possible ...

This is the darkest night yet ... Death alone could find his way in here now ... Thought I saw him sitting in that corner last night, waiting ... Yes ... He is there again-tonight ... I cannot see him ... But he is breathing softly, and I hear him ... It is funny to think of Death breathing ... Perhaps if it were not so still he would not be heard ... He will sit there all night ... He may come and stand over me as he did last night ... If he does, I shall ask him ... I feel him coming towards me, not walking, but, as it were, floating, like smoke in the air ... listlessly.

'Well, Death, how goes it?'

'Better with me than with you.'

'You are judging by men's bodies, Death. It is by their souls these men are living.'

'But I am concerned only with the body. Since man was, the earth has looked to me to feed it with bodies. That I have done. Not recently in Ireland as generously as in other places. But here my day is coming. I smell it in the winds that prophesy. The soul is nothing. There are no deeper greens for grass in the soul, no broader blades.'

'There will be no deeper greens from our bodies, Death; no broader blades … Our bodies will soon be only our souls.'

'Bones are the best manure. These I shall get in full. They will be ready dressed for the white tongues of the grass.'

'But you are not a master, Death; you are a servant. What you get you give to the earth or to the sea; but you cannot order. You have to wait until we are given to you, wait for the rejected of the tables of God.'

'God is my Master, but He trusts me. He has found me a good servant. Seldom He interferes with my work. He will not interfere now. His interference was in the days when I was inexperienced. The world called them miracles. They were simply my mistakes corrected by the Master of my craft. The period of my apprenticeship is long gone by. The age of miracles is passed,' the people say. And I cherish the phrase always and love those who say it. It is a high tribute to me.'

'What are your methods, Death?'

'I have only one method. Whether I am to come soon or late, I do not decide. He decides. But when I am come time ceases. It is given to me to enter in even to the souls of those to whom I am sent. The man whom I am taking knows, before any others know, that I am taking him. For I am in him even when those whom you call doctors are smiling with vanity at their own achievements. No man I take unawares. They all know. Many feel they are dying who do not die. But none know they are dying who do not die. And none know until I am come; and once I am come, I never leave without my body for the dry, brown earth. People there have been who have written of death. These do not know. If they had known they could not have written. When I have come into a man, I close his senses one by one. That sense which he gratified most I leave him longest. If it be the great things of the mind which he cherished, his mind lives even while his body lies dead. If it be his flesh which he nursed in desire, then his flesh dies last and the fires of its yearnings torture him. As I quench one by one the candles of his life there is no time. Sudden death is a phrase of the living who do not know. Because a man falls and is dead, they think the calculated plan of death has not been worked out within him. To him, as to you who are to die interminably, there is the same death given.'

'And when the last sense comes to be closed, the last candle quenched?'

'It is then that man struggles with me. In fairness I have left to him the power for which he most desires to live, for which he will fight most resolutely. The struggle is often very hard and bitter and long; but it is in that struggle that death begins and ends.'

'In that struggle you always win?'

'I always win; for that struggle always kills. Death is the robbing from man of his great desire.'

'But if a man's great desire be unity with God: what then?'

'Then he does not struggle. His senses are extinguished one by one, but I cannot rob him of his great desire. That which he yearns for is given him in death.'

'Is such a man, then, never afraid of death?'

'All men are afraid of me. My Master was afraid of me, of the powers He had given me. It is the humanity in man which dreads my coming, although the divinity in him has prayed for my coming. But death deals only with the humanity in man, and the soul is inundated with the fear that is in the flesh. My Master was perfect as a Man; and His manhood, the more intensely for its perfection, abhorred my coming.'

'And what of those who lose consciousness and meet you without waking?'

'The knowledge of death is in the flesh. All who meet me are awake, because they are not dead. Consciousness is a human word and has no real meaning.'

'When … when you are come to speak with men, are you … are you come to enter them?'

'Not always.'

'Are you come to enter me?'

'Not yet.'

'Are you come to enter any here?'

'Not yet.'

'Then why are you come?'

'I am come because there are many who yearn for me to enter them.'

'Many of the men here?'

'Yes, many. At nights they have cried out for me. But I am not ordered and cannot come. But soon, soon I shall be ordered. I have sat in the cells with all these men. I am sitting in the cell of each now, answering strange questions. They have begun to look with a great friendliness upon me. At first they were afraid and covered their faces when I came. Now there is kindliness for me in their eyes. I learn most from the eyes. I shall soon be ordered.'

'What if you are not ordered?'

'I shall go away.'

'Will you feel, as men say you feel – cheated?'

'I am never cheated. I enter and men die. If I do not enter, men live for a time – a little time. But I enter always and each man dies. I who entered Adam have learned to wait with patience. I who entered Christ have learned to wait with confidence.'

He is gone ... 'Death!' ... He does not answer ... 'Death! ... There is more I must ask you, Death ... more ... What is beyond you? How do you take the body and leave the soul? With what sense am I to fight the battle you will win? ... Why don't you answer, Death? ... Even you in the cell are better than darkness that has no beginning and no end.' ...

The doctors said we cannot live more than one other night ... Surely they could put a light in the cells tonight ... It wouldn't cost them so much ... It is black, black ... I was talking to Death ... This is not ordinary darkness ... The doctors told the Governor that tonight some of us would be dead ... I heard Death's voice too clearly to make a mistake ... It is close, too, no light, no air ... Something near me all round ... Almost touching me ... touching my face, too ... I must not scream ... but ... I am in my coffin ... Coffined ... No wonder Death would tell me his secrets … And he said he had not come to take us yet … He could have spoken the truth … I won't show the white feather … I suppose he was afraid of a scene …

… I must not feel for the sides … There is hope so long as I am not sure … Surely they have not nailed down the lid … that would be so cowardly … when we have not the strength to break it … They think we are dead … Or perhaps they know that we shall not live and they are saving themselves trouble in the morning … curs! It must have been when I was speaking with Death … They put me in then … I hope it is a plain coffin … Brass is shabby on coffins … Wonder is there a plate, and what have they put on it? 'Frank,' I suppose. 'Frank' will look so cheap on a coffin-plate …

Perhaps we are all in one coffin … Ah! that would be horrible. All rolling to one end as the foot of the coffin, or head, were raised … The cold, damp face of Ryan pressing on mine … We won't submit to this; they will have to give us a coffin each or build partitions in this one. We should have put that in our demands … The others will blame me for forgetting it … Perhaps those who like one another could put their arms round one another before they die and not roll … When it comes very near the end I must tell them that … More raving! God, You must give me strength to hold my mind from these thoughts. You know I am willing to die if death it must be. Let me not die like this every night, a score of times every night, wildly, pitifully … Yet, when Your hour was drawing near, You were sorrowful … Perhaps there is mercy in this madness …

There is not to be sleep even tonight … Seven days awake and seven nights! Heigh-ho, but we shall all be soon asleep and it will be hard to waken us …

A poem? That went well last night …

Let the sun, let the sun slip through the day,
Building gold roads through the unbuilt green,
Steeping far hills in the blue of the bay …

'Unbuilded green' … 'scene' … 'screen' … 'mean' … 'e'en.' 'E'en,' that suggests things, but the word itself is forced. 'Preen' … 'sheen' … 'Sheen,' bad as a word also, otherwise there could be possibilities … 'Keen' … 'clean' … 'lean' … 'been' … 'queen.' … 'Queen' … the moon? … No, I must start something new … Yes, a death ode to all of us … I shall try that.

The people have a cowed and frightened air,
And there is dread even in children's eyes:
But some young men are standing here and there,
In theirs the strange white fire that never dies.
And now and then there comes the half-screamed prayer.
Of some poor soul whom madness deifies.

The great gates open wide: men's heads are bare
As a plain coffin comes; and, like a prise,

Is claimed with breathless horror everywhere:
But many coffins follow and the wise
Pass from the place to some white altar near.

The riding coffins fret the redd'ning skies.
An old, grey man asks of a young man near
To call the names; and from the answer flies;
A young girl takes bright riband from her hair.

The rules have a cowed and frightened air,
And there is dread only in tyrants' eyes;
Young men and old are marching everywhere,
In theirs the strange white fire that never dies.


As a poet I may prove to be a good prophet … Two lines seem to be good: 'A young girl takes bright riband from her hair' is the expression of a whole people's spontaneous sorrowing; and 'The wise pass from the place to some white altar near' gives both the mental terror of the scene and the only hope left.

## Wednesday, April 14th, 1920

Must not forget what Philip told me today. Men in the hospital are being tempted to eat ... If the hospital warder – a friend – thinks it necessary, I am to collapse and be taken there to reorganise the place. Hope it will not be necessary ...

Wish Philip had selected some other job for me. I hate having to collapse ... I shall do it badly, blushing and perspiring and stuttering over any explanation I give ... It is not the lying which worries me so much as the feeling that the doctors will know ... I shall be caught out in a mean pretence, and for years after it the thing will surge back into my memory, stinging me with humiliation, leaving me hot and cold, red-faced and confused ... The day when I said 'compromiss' instead of 'compromise' still burns in me ... I see the room in which the tragedy of error occurred and feel the cold eye of Mrs French, then an unretired schoolmistress, on me still ... Mrs French is dead now ... It must be fifteen years ago ... And that awful mistake with Frances ... That was the worst ... When I am an old man I shall feel that just as keenly as today ... And now Philip says I must pretend to have collapsed if any of the men in hospital have taken food ...

Hallo! somebody has really collapsed ... They are opening a door hurriedly, noisily ... On this side of the ward ... Two doors ... More than one has collapsed ... My God! ... That's O'Neill's door, Shanahan's, Ellis' ... Good heavens! Philip's door ... And Twomey's ... I am alone ... I must run this strike to the end, the horrible, limp end ... .men cursing me for a stubborn fool, dying men cursing me ... Day after day I must say 'No,' 'No,' 'No' ... And for each 'No' a man will die ... God, You can give me strength to do what is right, give it! You said, Ask, and you shall receive: I ask for courage and sanity for myself and all here ... They have opened Murphy's door too ... It is the sudden end the doctors feared ... They are coming this way ...

... But surely so many could not have collapsed ... It is some message, some message the warders are bringing ... A general release? ... It might be ... It *is* ... The strike is won, won, WON ... We are to live ... They are letting us out now so that there will be no demonstration outside; when the streets are empty; when Curfew has cleared every soul indoors ... They are clever in their defeat ... Yes, it is surely release ... They have opened almost every door and have left them open, while the men get ready, I suppose ... Oh! Jesus, thanks ... The criminals are grumbling at the noise ... They'd wish us 'Good luck' if they knew ... Here they come ...

'Hallo! What is it?'

'Cell doors to be left open all night; doctor's orders.'

'Oh!'

Cell doors open all night? ... Regulations have admitted defeat at last ... Doctor's orders! If any man collapses now he will be so far gone that they must not waste a moment ... That is what 'doctor's orders' means ... The doctors are in a panic at night just as we are ... They have my sympathy ...

The wind is howling outside ... Death's wind that prophesies? ... It is sweeping through the passages and into the cells ... It is very cold ... We shall all get pneumonia out of this ... But at least it is not as dark as it was ... Yet what little relief the light is now that we know we can have it ... The stillness has left the prison too; there are footsteps everywhere and the murmur of men talking ... I wish they would shut the doors and let us die in peace ... It is very cold ...

That is 'Gay' talking. Seventeen-and-a-half 'Gay' is,

they say ... He is speaking from his bed ... suffering is evident from his voice ...

'Philip?'

'Yes. Is that you, Gay?'

''Tis ... The doctor was here an hour ago with brandy. I refused it.'

'That's right: no brandy.'

'He says I'm dying. I told him that as long as I'm not dead it didn't matter.'

'Good lad, Gay; that's the talk.'

'Philip?'

'Yes, Gay.'

'He wanted to put a mustard plaster over my heart.'

'But you are allowed to have that done, Gay. Other men have them.'

'Oh! but Philip, mustard is food and it might soak in.'

'Gay?'

'Yes.'

'Orders are to take the mustard plaster. Do you hear?'

'Yes, Philip, but ...'

'Gay,' I said, 'Orders are orders.'

'I suppose I must take it so.'

'Philip?'

'Yes, Gay.'

'The hospital warder said I should take a pill.'

'Well?'

'I told him I was on hunger-strike.'

'Gay?'

'Yes.'

'Orders are to take the pill. Do you hear?'

'I do; but this is a queer kind of hunger-strike.'

The Northern men who came in last Thursday and joined the hunger-strike then are walking around the passages. They look very big in the shadow light ... They are talking now ...

'Wully.'

'Yass.'

'Thon's lack Balfas' pressan, eh?'

'Yass; it'd be lack it.'

'Wully' is away at the other end of the ward. But distance is no hindrance to the conversation. They are all calling 'Wully' now ... 'Wully' seems to be popular ... But none of us will be able to sleep if this goes on ...

'Hallo, boys!'

'Yass.'

'Better go back to bed and try to sleep. Some of our lads want sleep very badly, and this talking will keep them awake.'

'Wully.'

'Yass.'

'Yer to stap talkin'.'

Poor 'Wully'! He had said hardly anything ...

It is very draughty and cold. I suppose the light makes a difference ... We are not to die in the dark, after all ... But if men die tonight all the others will know ... It will make them all nervous ... The hearts will stop then ... It is curious that none of them grumble at dying like this ... Even the real soldiers amongst them ... Indeed all ... They are all Volunteers ... dying like this must seem horrible to them ... They see, I suppose, that prisoners can't be choosers ...

Good heavens! ... Must tell that to Philip. What a chance it is! ... The men would jump at it ... It would give them all strength enough to come except Brennan and one or two others ... Then we could all die as soldiers ... Tomorrow night, if the releases have not begun, it must be done ... Death will be certain for us all then ... The men might as well have the opportunity of dying as Volunteers ... It will be a terrible adventure ... The sensation it will cause outside! ... And the guard may not fire ... We would all be put in handcuffs and strait-jackets when it was over ... That would be all for the best ... It would horrify our own people and other nations too ... It might break the Castle ... If the guard does fire (and we must be prepared for that), and men are shot down they will have to release the others who live ... Must plan this out carefully and

have it watertight for Philip. He will be critical at first ...
But he will agree and be the man who will lead it ...

The open cell-doors give us the chance ... We shall
tell the men to arm themselves with legs from their tables,
silently broken, arm themselves with anything at all ...
After midnight, when most of the warders are gone home,
Philip will give the order ... Some of us had better steal
out first and manage the warders ... There are three here
tonight: there will not be more tomorrow night ... If the
same men are on, Neville and O'Shea would surrender
easily. The other, McSharry, is bitter and would give trouble. He had better be called into a cell and tied up there ...
Philip and I could go into the same cell and do it ... He will
have the keys of the gates ... When the warders are down,
forty men at least will come with us ... The Northerners
are strong still ... 'Wully', if his voice is any indication,
will be invaluable ... We shall creep down the stairs to the
ground-floor ... Twomey and Sam and one of the Newry
men are big enough to wear the warders' clothes and do
the opening of the gates for the others ... It will help to
confuse any official onlookers ... Warders will seem to be
bringing us somewhere ... If the preliminaries are carried
out quietly it would work ... We can get out past the office
easily enough ... And then ... then the guard ... We must
rush them at once ... They might with the unexpectedness

of it, with fright at the weird sight of us, dishevelled, haggard, mad-looking, queerly clothed, moving unnaturally owing to our weakness ... they might give up their rifles not knowing where they were or what was happening ... But if they use them the men will be prepared for that too ... If they shoot us down the thing will ring all over the world ... It would be the greatest service the Republic has yet been given ... And it is so easy ... so much easier than dissolving here ... It could be done now ... I have always felt that I shall die by shooting ... The premonition may be fulfilled tomorrow night ... But it will be a quick warm death ... The excitement of silencing the warders ... the trooping down the polished iron steps to meet death, the stealing through silent passages to it ... We shall be so fired with it all that we shall not feel our wounds ... I hope Philip will see as I see ... Tomorrow night hope will be gone ... We can afford to take desperate courses ... If he agrees he will laugh when leading us out past the office to face the guard ... I am trembling with excitement ... It seems so wasteful to have to wait until tomorrow night ...

What, if when the moment comes I am afraid ... Death tomorrow is always acceptable if it be not certain ... But, death today, now ... that is different ... I shall not be afraid openly ... The others will not know ... I shall go first with Philip. It is I who have planned it and can claim that place

... Then I cannot turn back ... If I were in the last rank, I might stand still ... But in front ... I shall not want to turn back with Philip striding at my side, his face just a little harder. There will be strength for me in that ...

There must be rapture in dying as we shall die if the guard fires, in walking to death as the followers of every great cause have walked to it, not waiting for it: seeking it ... What a pride must have been in the early Christians as they trooped into the arena, wilfully ... Even the meaner types in the great circling crowd which they saw silhouetted against the sky must have sensed the exaltation of so militant a submission ... God uses the gentle in such strange ways ... It is always the gentle that He seems to use ...

I know some who will convince themselves from our worn bodies, by the wistfulness in our faces when we are dead, that no God exists ... They will not see that we are not the denial but the proof of God ... The strength we have from Him ... If there were no Spirit of Justice, how could It seek out our souls in this darkness and fight with them the injustice of man ... For the souls of men are the weapons of God ... With them He has done gentle battle down the ages, fierce gentle battle, in which only the victors die and the victory is in making the souls of the defeated also the weapons of God ... The thing we are doing now is the replacing of justice into hearts that have hardened themselves against it. That is what we are dying for ... A hundred of us, a mere handful of men being used as the proof that the things of the spirit are greater than the things of the flesh; and that the flesh must be offered up in defence of the spirit ... It is well that this thing has come now. A people is most moved by the power of sacrifice the soul creates in the body ... When we are dead we shall be an inspiration to the people. Men will live better because we have died – not many men: some in this city, some in that; a greater number in the villages and towns because there the spirit is not trampled out by the brute thing they call progress ... Pearse made many understand and love the Spirit of God and Its attributes justice and liberty ... love them with a zeal almost wanton ... Men who die in loneliness and darkness for that which is half-human, half-divine, a nation's tradition, these men light strange fires in the hearts of men and teach them the greatness of love and gentleness and the simple non-submission to evil ... This hunger-strike did not begin in a desire to teach this or any other thing. It began in the wilful intention to fight and defeat a tyranny which touched ourselves personally and the nation for which we are greatly ... It had personal gains in it also ... For me there was personal gain hidden in among the things which prompted me to strike ... But, liberty and justice, the fight for these overshadowed the sordid things

… That is true … It requires something greater than self to make a man willing to give up his life … Death is the proof a sceptical world demands of a man's love for justice, of the superiority of justice over life … The world does not understand the greatness of liberty until death is found in defending it … Many said they would believe in Casement if he were hanged … Ugh! … Sincere people who when Casement *was* hanged took inspiration from him …

Not through our choosing, our names have become with our people a synonym for their tradition, the tradition of tireless revolt against tyranny … Not this name or that but 'The Mountjoy Hunger-strikers' … It is better that way … Too long have unworthy names been great whispering words among our people … The many are forgotten because the few are named …

I wonder can our enemies know that by killing us they are creating a hundred thousand of us … History has told them that, Irish history more frequently than any other … They must never read history … Perhaps the people who make history never read it; perhaps if they read it they would not want to make it … The history of an empire is such a cowardly thing when it is understood … Subject peoples have few historians until they are free: that is strange too … It means that until a people is freed the class which has the leisure and the means which writing history implies is foreign to its own people; that the historian class is ashamed of its own people until by recognised freedom it becomes respectable ... And, yet, it is not so strange; for the learned are usually the sons of the well-to-do – in subject peoples at least – and well-to-do are themselves the sons of Mammon – not all, but many. And it is Mammon which enslaves and oppresses weak nations. It is really the historians' own fathers who are being written of by them; and it becomes akin to parricide for the historian of a subject people to champion its strivings for freedom ... Perhaps that is also why a people battling against imperial encroachment is led by men of great character and great ability; but not often of great culture ... Here, too, may be the reason why a people when it becomes free becomes materialistic: when freedom is won the class which reverences respectability has no longer reason to malign its nation so it leads it; leads it to the worship of Mammon, the only deity the respectable class has ever really understood ... This was never so clear to me as now when those who are doing battle for us outside are the waitresses and quayworkers; while many who are called cultured and learned are cursing the closed doors of a favourite club ...

My thoughts are peaceful tonight, even-running, simple thoughts ... The fear of death has gone ...

Perhaps it will come back before the night is passed and the new day begins with its round of doctors and newspapers and friends and shadows and far-away singing … and after it all the wonderful stillness of Curfew … But I shall be more ready to meet the fear when it comes … much more ready … I have a calmness all tonight that I cannot understand … Yet I have no hope … It may be God's mercy making it easy for us …

Oh! … I am afraid … It has all come back … come back wildly, suddenly … Why did I think of my calmness? … The horror is beginning again, the madness is coming back … I would run and run if I could, anywhere, away from my thoughts … I feel it all, fear, despair, doubt, revulsion … I cannot do anything to stop it now … It has me in its black arms … I have tried so often to resist it and have failed … I am tired of trying …

Yes, it's the only way … The Dáil must declare the strike off; must order us all to stop striking … A note to MC … I will ask Philip to send a note to Mick Collins to have the Ministry issue a statement calling off the strike … They can say that the enemy Government have planned our deaths, not that they may keep their prisoners in prison, but that they may get the people into the streets, into position for the Amritsar. To prevent that immeasurable tragedy the Ministry calls upon the Mountjoy

Hunger-strikers to take food … That must be done now, at once … at once …

So it has got as far as this … my suggesting surrender, meanly suggesting it, trying to escape the odium of it by putting the surrender into other mouths … There will be no note to Mick Collins … We went into this thing with our eyes open and we will stay in it until we have won or have taken the consequences … Besides, we told the men on the first day of the strike that nothing would be permitted to break it: told them that we had consulted G.H.Q., that G.H.Q. left the decision to us and would support us whatever it was … Warned the men that when the strike had gone a certain distance G.H.Q. might try to stop it, and it was unanimously agreed that no person or no organisation would be permitted to interfere … How glad I am now that we thought of that! It closes the one remaining avenue of escape … We must go on, on, on … Myself and the others who are brave … Coward with men of courage, coward leading men of courage … Ha! Ha! …

No, that is not true … I counted the cost and accepted it … accepted it in the distance when I did not understand what it would mean … but, I accept it still, now, when I know it means everything horrible … I have my internal revolutions, a kind of personal Mexico … But the great outstanding fact of death I accept … That is true; I feel that that is true ... that I will not shirk death ... If there were an honourable way of escape, I should be glad: I shall not hide that either; I should be very glad; ... But at times I am glad there is no escape. Ireland needs a revolution. Easter Week has to be repeated that the people may realise their subjection; for, once they realise it, it is over, they will end it ... That is in my mind every time I look into Philip's face ... That cleansing revolution may be at hand if we have courage ...

My heart has stopped beating ... It is the end ... I think I am glad ... I think ... But I can't die like this! Surely I am not to die like this ... Weak and frightened and pitiful. Somebody must come ... I must call ... 'Hallo!' ... I cannot even hear myself ... God, what a death this is to be! ... If only I could go to the door ... But it will not be long now ... Oh! what a horrible thing death is! ... Cannot somebody come? ... No, there must be no panic ... If I make a noise dying, I shall frighten the others ... Must die quietly as any of the others would ... Good-bye everybody ... M— and F— and C— most of all ... God, if I have done wrong in this let Your great Heart find mercy in it for me ... I thought I would be glad to die ... I should like to be glad to die ... The light is fading ... I am losing my sight ... I wish I were glad ... I ...

There has been some change ... What is it? ... It wasn't

as dark as this ... My hands are wet ... wet and cold ... clammy and cold, as if they had played a trick on me and died before me ... My forehead is damp too and icy cold when the wind passes me ... Something has happened and I don't know what it is ... It is something horrible or why should I be wet all over like this? ... Yes, I heard Gay talking ... Gay has a nice face ... And then everybody was walking in the passages ... making noise ... speaking ... Ah! yes; the Northern men ... They're lucky, coming in late like this; we'll be dead before them and they'll get out then. Wish I had come with the Northern men ... And ... perhaps it is stopped still ... perhaps I *am* dead ... It is quiet ... dark ... no stir ... The doors were open ... no doors now, no voices now ... Yet there is a breeze somewhere ... my forehead feels it ... It wouldn't feel it if ...

Only another panic ... another of the many deaths ... They have shut the cell-doors again; that is why it is so still and strange ... Another night is nearly over and I am alive still ... When I thought I was dying, the longing became terrible, the longing to be glad to die; and just when the darkness tightened around my mind as if somebody were working at it with a wrench I felt glad, joyously glad ... Saw that this is almost the ideal death, with the fires of the flesh gone out and the soul so close to God ... to give up our lives that a people's right to be free might be re-spoken to the world ... I knew, rapturously knew, just as the full weight of nothingness was bolted down upon me, that of us too it would be said: 'They shall be remembered for ever' ...

Somebody walking on the floor above us ... A warder ... They are opening the doors again ... It may be near dawn ...

'What is the hour, please?'

'Twenty-five to four.'

'Why are you opening these again?'

'Shouldn't have been shut. Some of your lads complained of the cold and we shut them. Doctor has come in, kicked up a row and they are being opened again.'

'There is a regular gale blowing through the place ... the rise and fall of the wind is like somebody keening us, like everybody in Ireland keening us ...

That's Murphy coughing, a racking cough ... it tears my throat too ... It must leave him very weak ... I suppose all the others are awake also ... I see them – that blue transparency in their faces which fasting gives, big wide eyes with a steady stare in them, lips tightly pressed together ... In behind the hardness of their faces perhaps their minds too are on fire like mine, each believing that he alone is afraid to die, that all the others laugh and are joyful at the darkening of the shadows, that only he is a coward ... Oo-oo-oo! ... Cold wind ... It is getting into my bones ...

Wish they'd shut the doors: darkness would be better than cold … Gold will help to kill us … If they would shut the door, I wouldn't hear Murphy coughing … It makes me want to vomit … They should take him to hospital … Ah! aaah! the man will kill himself … No other sound in the whole jail but Murphy tearing at his throat … Where are the warders? … Why don't they walk around and not make us think we are in a morgue with one of the corpses not quite dead coughing what remains of himself away …

The dawn at last … Sweetest sight of the whole day … It is something greater than joy to be able at last to distinguish between the white wall and the black door and then to watch the light grow and grow and to know that day is here again and dying has become easy.

That porridge … Who cares whether it is wasted or not so long as we can smell it … breathe it in … I could put my arms around the man who makes it … What would I not give to be standing over it now, stirring it, feeling the steam in my face! …

'How are the others, Warder?'

Many collapsed … Five taken to hospital … Five … I heard none going … Maybe in the few minutes after my heart had stopped beating they were brought away … It might have been the testing hour for all of us …

They say that Bonar Law has said we must die ... Very well, Mr Law ... You must keep your Empire; but we must keep our faith. And our faith will outlast your Empire ... You think you are dealing with less than a hundred prisoners in but one of the thousand jails upon which your Imperial domination rests ... But numbers are nothing and men are nothing ... You are dealing with an old nation's tradition, its memory, its destiny, its faith ... You are dealing with the boyhood of the world: a young Ireland, a young India, a young Egypt, and perhaps even, Mr Law, a young England. We are merely the manifestation of an ancient nation's immortality and a young world's hatred of injustice and oppression ... What can you do against elemental things? ... Kill? ... But killing spreads a faith and we are become a faith. By letting us die you make unknown men known to every lover of liberty, intimately known ... so intimately known that our names shall have an influence without bounds of space or time ... It is a glad day for us, Mr Law, that you make us die; and a proud day for our people ...

The hospital orderly has been in with a little note from Philip: 'Have just had word from McCrane who went to hospital last night that all the men over these are holding firm and that Cullen has stopped tempting them. No need for you to go over so. How do you feel?'

How do I feel? As if a load had been taken off me. The orderly looked surprised at the smile I gave ... He will put all kinds of wrong constructions on it ... So long as I haven't to pretend to be worse than I am, he can think what he likes ...

Have seen today's papers ... Hardly any other news but of us. No need to complain of lack of publicity ... Erskine has seen to that ably ... The headings of the *Independent* are almost a record of the national excitement ... 'Prisoners sinking rapidly' ... 'Pitiable Position' ... 'Further Militaristic Displays' ... 'Barbed Wire at Jail' ... 'Aeroplanes over Dublin yesterday' ... 'Enormous Assembly' ... 'Machine Guns on Prison Walls' ... 'Determination of Prisoners' ... 'Splendid discipline of people' ... The General Strike is in operation all over the country, business of all kinds being suspended ... But the British are evidently as determined that it shall go on as the people are that it shall stop ... The *Independent* in its leader says the Government has 'banged, barred and bolted the doors' ... 'No other Government would be so conscienceless as to set at defiance such a national protest' ... Undoubtedly the two nations are at death-grips ... Last night tens of thousands of people were singing and praying outside these walls ... We are become the vanguard of the whole race as it marches, stubbornly, mechanically almost, so fixed is its resolution, against the massed power of the Empire ... The papers are full of rumours, too, of probable concessions, but the British Government will never so speedily eat their strong words of yesterday ... They will offer us less than we demand and we must not take it ... Outside too they are expecting deaths: 'some sinking rapidly, death might take place any moment' ... Hope that when it does the discipline of the people will last ... We are on the eve of a mighty thing; of something which has not happened before to our nation ... Though I know deep, deep in me that it is right and just and good for us to die, I cannot kill the fear of dying ... Sometimes I am not sure which is deeper ... the dread of dying or the sorrow of not dying ... If the will could hold the imagination, keep the mind in subjection, crush out the million tiny fears and doubts and frightened impulses which swarm and swarm like ants over a corpse in the desert – then it would be easy ... But the will, though strong enough to make death certain, itself is overwhelmed by this invisible terror ...

What if God condemns us when we go to Him? ... Oh! horror! All this is bearable because He surely is with us ... But is He? If He be not, then come madness, terror, every crooked phantom and take reason from me before I realise that He is against us ... If He is, we must yield ... No! No! No! Things have reached that pitch now that we must face the anger of God rather than give in; suffer even in our souls for the freedom of our people … But it would be futile to serve an ideal, to seek any good, in opposition to Him; or to expect to raise up our nation by evading His Will … If He be against us, then this strike will fail if it succeeds; and surrender, with all its bitterness and seeming betrayal of the people, betrayal just in the very moment of victory, will be the truer path to freedom … God give me strength to yield if Your Will is not being done in this …

But I thought all this out before … These are only the same mad doubts which crowd and crowd and crowd, endlessly, devilishly, without a shred of mercy … God is Truth, and Liberty is part of Truth, and to serve Liberty is to serve God. The Saints died to profess Liberty. There are no other means to free our people than those we are using now … they are just and honourable means … If I weren't weak and wasted physically, I wouldn't have having these fears …

They are calling a 'Stop Press' in the streets … What has happened? … Have they yielded? … Or, more likely, has someone died? … the first of us … the head of the file …

Kells has been shot dead! Kells … Good heavens! At his garden gate … I suppose he had his hat on the side of his head, jauntily on the side of his head as he had this day fortnight when he walked down our line trying to pick men out for the gallows … He is dead now … I see the horrible scene of that day all over again ... The double file of troops as they tramped into the exercise ring ... The belief that the twenty of us chosen from the others were to be deported ... Our shouted promise to carry the strike wherever he went ... Our march through the Wing singing the 'Soldiers' Song', swinging along, led by Philip, the song, wonderful in the echoes the building gave it, making tingling wine of our blood ... And then, suddenly, as we swung out of the main entrance and into the wood-yard, Philip's startled cry: 'Keep your heads down, lads. The windows! Identification parade' ... Which tore my eyes to the windows, high above the yard, and where I saw wild eager eyes, bright vengeful bitter eyes peering horribly down at us ... darting here and there seeking some better vantage-place to find the faces they sought ... wolves, hyenas ... that was the impression ... I have it still, of those sinister, shadowy, stealthy figures with glazing eyes, moving queerly behind those windows ... Then the sudden recollection that I should have my head down ... Philip ordered us to line up under the windows so that we could not be seen from them ... Half an hour passed as the balked 'spotters' sought another way ... Then the quick darting past and glancing in of men and women from the top of the wood-yard's downward steps ... sudden, swift, flitting movements to prevent recognition by us ... Finally Philip's warning that 'G'-men were coming, and his order that any who recognised particular men should call out their names ... The group of 'G'-men at the top of the steps, keeping their backs to us – for spies were beginning to learn that theirs was a dangerous calling – reluctant to come close enough to see, lest that mean close enough to be seen ... The fat one who kept trying to look round without turning round ... Remember counting the creases in his neck ... And then the figure with the jaunty hat and the waterproof over the left arm who detached himself from the group ... came down the steps, slowly ... halted ... then walked forward along our line, studying each face as he passed, his eyelids half-closed to help his peering, a sneer on his lips ... I noticed that his blue serge suit was old but well brushed ... Like a shot a cry from our line: 'Aha! Kells, is this the work you are on? Look out' ... An angry snarl from the rest of us ... Kells, paler, with the jaunty air and the curled lips gone from him, went back up the steps ... by obvious willpower getting himself to halt now and again lest he give the appearance of hurrying ... The identification parade was over ... We sang on the way back too ...

And now Kells is dead ... Shot dead this morning ... The news unnerves me a little ... He and I may see one another before long ... Shall we have anything to say? ... War is a bestial thing ... It is so much greater to give your life than to take another's ... Great Lord! I remember the footnote of a letter from M— to Philip yesterday ... 'I am going to Kells tomorrow' ... A coincidence? ... More likely an intimation, daringly given ...

The strike is certain to continue now ... French, in face of Kells' death, could not possibly make terms ... So carefully does it seem that every chance of settlement is being nipped in the bud – it must be our destiny to die ...


The Lord Mayor is in the prison, the warders say ... If so, the strike is won ... That is what it means if it be true ... I will not believe that he is here ... It will sap my strength to go on if I build up hopes of settlement like this ... Since one o'clock the prison has been humming with rumours of a surrender by the Government ... Have cautioned any who came near me to put the very thought of it out of their heads ...

Philip and Twomey have been here and the whole situation has completely changed ... The Governor has offered 'political treatment' to all prisoners ... I want to accept, if his definition of political treatment – it has not been defined yet – gives us the rights of prisoners-of-war ... Philip is against this ... He says he will take nothing less than release now ... I reminded him of our demand and read him a copy of the ultimatum the three of us served on the Governor on April 1st:

The undersigned, acting on behalf of all untried and uncharged prisoners, hereby demand that on or before the morning of April 5th all such prisoners be released or given prisoner-of-war treatment.

Philip said that bound us to take prisoner-of-war treatment instead of release before April 5th, but not after it … He added that, no matter who accepted 'political treatment,' he was carrying on for release …

So strongly led, Twomey and I followed impulsively … This was a new fight; but Philip said with fire in his eyes: 'We have them beaten and we'll make them take a defeat, not an arrangement.'

They both went out … the cell door closed slowly because Twomey has become very weak and moves feebly … Philip looks just as when I spoke to him in the ring, years ago it seems now, but his face is whiter and the skin tightly drawn upon it … We are all beginning to look like dressed-up skulls.

… I was mad to agree with Philip … mad … We shall fail now, surely … The strike is won with their offer of political treatment … If they refuse to release us, it is lost, utterly lost … for the men will not die now that the alternative demand has been granted … I should have known better … It has at last become a mere playing with lives, with the lives of Brennan's children … We could be taking food now if I had not agreed ... taking back life ... drinking and eating hope and the pride of having won ... And because Philip has conceived some wild plan we must go on stinking here ... in the day dreading the night, in the night dreading the day ... blaming God for not letting us sleep and being afraid that He will let us and that we shall not wake again ... knowing that all who love us outside are suffering more keenly than we are, infinitely more ... that they are living on the rack, the rack that twists and tortures the mind, the rack that breaks not bones, but hope and faith and love ... that they are living like that from moment to moment, wanting to scream, yet all the time being queerly silent, like someone whose mind is dead ... And for what? ... That Philip may have his fad ... We have won, and we mustn't take our victory until we have gone out of this imbeciles, drivelling imbeciles all of us ... So that when our people see us they will whisper and nod and shake their heads and ... they put us into asylums and forget us ... All because Philip has had an idea ... I'll go to him and tell him ... What do I care for him? ... I won't look at his face ... I will say ...

Erskine and Denis and a fair-haired Australian priest have been here ... They congratulated me on our having won ... They don't know what has happened ... They say the people are wild with joy ... Erskine said nothing at all … Sat on the end of the mattress and looked at me … smiling wonderfully whenever our eyes met … dear Erskine … I must have rambled away at them, for I did not understand the questions they asked me … They were here a long time … Denis was talking a lot … I wanted Erskine to talk, but he didn't … The fair-haired priest asked me would I receive Communion … Felt appalled: I was not prepared: my thoughts were so far from Him … Forget what answer I made … I remember he put his arm about me when I made it … They don't know that the strike is to go on … Philip mustn't have said anything yet …

The Governor seems to believe that we are accepting his political treatment; for we are to be released on parole that our strength may be built up … Six weeks' parole, they say. Denis said there were motorcars and ambulances outside the gates ready to take us away, and that the cordon of troops and the tanks have been withdrawn … We are to go out at six, he said … Ha! Ha! … He doesn't know … nobody knows … The Australian priest said there are tremendous crowds around the jail … All day I heard the murmur of their prayers, then the snarl of some anti-English song, deep-throated, full of power, terrible power … There is cheering outside now … These people have beaten an Empire … even if we are going to take their victory from them …

I have seen Philip ... It was queer going ... shuffling ... along the passages ... holding on to the wire-caging ... glancing into cells to see little groups, happy groups who had gathered in some of the cells to talk out the glorious news, which was much more to them than food ... To see them, bright-faced, and to know that with a word I could bring back the pain and madness into those eyes! ... They don't know yet ... If they agree, but only if they agree, we will reject the offer of release on parole and accept only unconditional release ... Philip has convinced me that this is right to do; that it is not ourselves which concern us, but the nation, the people ... for them the jails must be opened and the jailing stopped ... I should have seen this myself ... I did see it when the strike started, and in all its dark hours until now ... Now Philip has had to say it to me ... As he said it, I knew it was he who was right and told him that, reddening as if I had deserted him under fire ... But that the strike may go forward after our refusal with the same strength with which it began, each man is to decide freely whether he will come the rest of the road with us ... only the willing ones must come ...

That talk with Philip makes him something new to me ... The hardness left his face ... for the first time left his face as he contrasted our duty to ourselves and our duty to the nation. A different light came into his eyes ... the steely sparkle of the pure militarist left them … What he said was wonderfully simple and true … 'It is the people's life, Frank, not ours,' was the last thing he said …

The plan is a daring one … good strategy … The Governor is evidently sure that political treatment plus parole will be accepted … He has made all arrangements for our removal before he tells us … Have to smile when I think of his official mind trying to grasp this new mystery … The ambulance will be outside, the private cars, the people … and we will not go! … The thing may succeed by its very rashness … But there is all the difference between releasing us on parole and unconditional release … Our present silence will give the thing the appearance of a trick … The Viceroy and those about him will have hardened from the death of Kells … If they have one good psychologist amongst them, he can tell them that the granting of political treatment must divide our forces, has already thrown open a road along which doubts and selfishnesses can enter anyone who fears death too much … If they are wise they will put us to the test … The certainty of death, coupled with the disappointment which the renewal of the strike must mean, may be too much for men after another sleepless night or two …

Have been round with Philip and Twomey to the men … The majority shamed me with the readiness with which they threw themselves into the new fight once Philip had explained … Before that, when they heard Philip say the strike was to go on, it was like studying the face of a man dying in torment to watch their expressions … Sometimes they were jollily making plans for tomorrow … tomorrow, free … when we came in … and the laughter went out of them as if something monstrous had suddenly passed in front of the sun … Heard a sharp intake of breath as Philip said it would not take long to win the whole thing … a day or two, as if to say, 'A day or two … why can't you be honest and say a night or two?'

The jail is as quiet as an empty church … a kind of quietness that is all suppression … Before our pilgrimage the noise of feet in the passages, men calling happily to one another, soft laughter and even a song … Now each man is again in bed … beginning the horrible fight all over again …

The Governor has been here and is gone … stupefied. He laughed when he came in. 'At last something you can accept, gentlemen,' he said, and a weight seemed lifted off him … I sent for Philip and Twomey. He chatted pleasantly with me while they were coming and wished a speedy recovery. He did not hide that he admired us. I think he even said he was glad we had won. Then Philip and Twomey came in … Smiling at us three, he read the official statement that we were to be released on parole and on our return to be given 'ameliorative treatment.' When he had finished he gave his little bow and said happily: 'I have ambulances outside for the worst cases and cars for the rest. We shall make a start in half an hour.' He took up his gloves to go …

Then Philip said – huskily, I thought: 'We will not accept parole; it must be unconditional release, or the strike goes on.'

There was a silence, as if somebody were pressing something sharp into my mind or playing an inaudibly shrill note, a silence that was physical torture …

The Governor looked this way and that … said nothing … His face became terribly old … He took down his monocle and stood slowly wiping it with a shaky handkerchief … looking fishily at Philip.

'But …' he said softly, then stopped … He coughed and said: 'But … you … demanded this … This is prisoner-of-war treatment. You can't refuse to accept it. I told them you would accept it. You asked me for it … I … I can't go back to …' He stopped again …

I felt guilty, as if we had tricked him. His look was like the look of a wounded animal, accusing us dumbly.

… I heard Philip's voice, hard, shrill … 'You or your masters let us go to death's door, and now offer us parole to come back and be killed at some time more suitable to them. You refused our demand ten days ago for the thing you now want us to take. You made us fight and we are fighting. And we are on top. Nothing less than unconditional release now. You forced us to face this rotten death. You can let us die if you like, and you then face the people.'

'But ...' said the Governor again, vacantly. Philip, weakened by the intensity with which he had spoken, swayed a little and clutched at the wall, breathing whistlingly through his nose, his lips tight-pressed, his eyes big and bright against the drawn skin ... He faced him ... type of all revolution facing the wizened, well-mannered Governor, lately a police-officer among some of the coloured peoples whom Britain oppresses ... this Governor who regarded all outside his class as 'native' – type of all Imperialism.

There was a pause ... then words came again ... 'They will never grant this. But I'll tell them what you say. It is very awkward ... I thought prisoner-of-war treatment was what you wanted.'

He turned to go. Philip said: 'You had better hurry. The doctors say men will surely die tonight.'

But after the first part of the sentence the Governor was gone ... Clearly his heart is not in it ... the whole thing terrifies him ... Excellent official; but a bad president of the rack ...

An hour ago he went ... There is no word yet ... The notice over the table has stared at me since he went:

# NOTICE

All persons committed to prison are informed that they will not be able by wilful injury to their bodily health, caused by refusal of food or in any other way, to procure their release before their discharge in the due course of law.

'In due course of law' ... crying law, law where there is no law. It is funny telling men imprisoned without charge or trial about the 'due course of law' ... Law has broken down ... Britain is frankly and professedly the malevolent despot ... and the more to be liked because part, at least, of the hypocrisy is gone.

'Will not be able ... to procure their release' ... Yes, it was a mistake to make release the only thing, the only acceptable thing ... This notice says nothing about prisoner-of-war treatment ... They would have yielded on that ... They *had* yielded on it ... If they just sat tight now and let the General Strike go on, how long could it last? ... Starvation would soon end it ... We have no right to risk the tremendous National defeat of the collapse of the General Strike ... Should have put it that way to Philip ... Can't say anything now ... The die is cast ... Die ... appropriate word ...

Wonder would I see a joke just on the point of death and want to laugh? ... It would be splendid to go out with an honest smile on one's lips ... The undertakers would be saved the trouble of making a beautiful expression ... A few deft movements of the fingers and – 'Oh! He died so peacefully; his face is lovely' ... The undertaker's boy probably knows how to do it, too – the little devil ... Part of the trade, perhaps! I'll try to make my own beautiful expression ... It would be ghastly to die raving ... with all the madness in the face ... the face distorted with it, so that Ruth would give a little scream and drop the cloth ... But the undertaker's boy would know how to retouch it ... to make it 'such a happy' face ... Curse the undertaker's boy ... I'll die mad if I like ... What business is it of his? ... Who the hell asked him to interfere ... brat ...

Have been out in the passages ... A few men moving about ... dragging their feet like very old men ... very, very old men ... Ha! Ha! we are all ancients ... old fellows ... patriots and patriarchs, both ... They'll release us when we have passed the age limit ... release a whole lot of thin little, old little, doting little men, who were robust, happy young men a fortnight ago ... I saw a warder out there ... Warder O'Kelly. Queer smile he gave me ... There is something in his eyes I don't like ... If he could hide it, people would be more friendly to him ... but nobody will tell him and he will go on looking like that all his life ... making people suspicious of him ... Thought I heard him say to O'Dowd, who looks ghastly: 'It's all up,' or something like that ... He mustn't be allowed to depress our lads ... It is hard enough for them ... He may be trying to break down our *morale*, sent in to do that ... Perhaps it is that I saw in his eyes ... If he went from cell to cell ... I will watch him ...

Warder O'Kelly is harmless, I think ... Just resting there, making no effort to speak to our lads ... As I watched him I saw Philip going round the landing below on some mission ... Wonder what it is? ... Merely looking for somebody, perhaps ...

Philip is going to run a concert ... Keep the men's mind off the waiting, he says ... 'Who'll sing?' I asked ... Some of the men just in ... Here's one of them ... Nice voice ... Lord what a song for a time like this!

> My young love said to me:
> My mother won't mind;
> And my father won't slight you
> For your lack of kind:
> And she laid her hand on me
> And this did she say:
> It will not be long, love, till our wedding-day.

Of all the weird airs! One of the Antrim ballads, I think ...

> She went away from me,
> And she moved through the fair;
> And fondly I watched her
> Move here and move there.
> And then she went homeward
> With one star awake
> As the swan in the evening moves over the lake.

He is singing it well: but the thing is a dirge ... It is getting on my nerves ...

> The people are saying
> That no two hearts were wed,
> But that one had a sorrow
> That never was said:
> And she smiled as she passed me
> With her goods and her gear,
> And that was the last that I saw of my dear.

Dead silence ... He stopped, and not one man clapped or cheered ... just dead silence ... It sounded awful ... Nobody has any hope ... That ends the concert ...

The latest word in is that French has turned down the release without parole and won't budge ... He has dared us, and the whole people through us ... We'll die ... He needn't be afraid ... He will get his pound of flesh ... I have that sinking inside, that queer physical fear ... 'Confession pains,' some genius called it ...

We are on our way to the great Confession ... That frightens me ... Dare we look God in the face? ... If Fr O'Carney is right, we go to Him suicides ... and those who led as murderers too, I suppose ... Dead because we were too proud not to die ... too concerned with what Miss This and Miss That would think and say of us ... Not much concerned with what He would think or say, until now ... But I no longer care ... I thought these things out once and the answer seemed right then; and if it was right then it is right now ... Why can't we die for liberty without monstrous doubts of this kind? ... Isn't liberty holy enough to die for? ... Or is the whole thing a farce from beginning to end? ... Some awful mad jest of God's? ... I don't know and I don't care ... I'm afraid to die, and I am going to die because I am afraid not to ... The papers will call me a hero and a martyr ... a miserable, frightened fool who hadn't the courage not to die ... And if anybody tells the truth about me after I'm dead they will hang him from the nearest lamppost ... Serve the fool right, too ...

Towards the end I suppose I'll howl and rave and give it all away ... 'The dying warrior' ... Ha! Ha! ... The Governor and his officials will stand by as I peter out, gabbling away, whimpering my reluctance to die and my cowardice not to die ... Perhaps they will take shorthand notes of what I say ... and publish it ... No! I will concentrate all the strength I have into dying silently ...

People are passing up and down outside, looking in ... I don't know them ... They are girls and men ... Must be going into some of the other cells ... Thought visitors were not let in after five ... They are not there when I look out ... When I lie down again they come back and make faces at me ... and laugh ... I hear them laugh and it is like a dentist's drill on a nerve ... They look quietly at me at first, and then suddenly burst into laughter ... When I say anything they run away, laughing, down the passages ... I hear only the girls laughing ... People should not be allowed to laugh out loud like that ... There they are again now ...

They make no noise coming ... They're just there ... As if you turned on a light and found them there ... looking in, over one another's shoulders ... Listen now and the girls will laugh ...

'What do you want?'

Do you hear? ... Did you ever hear such laughter? ... It pains like the sight of a wound ... They are all gone again ... down the passages ... to laugh at somebody else ... It should not be allowed ... They must know that we have got to die and will not be able to tell those outside what they have done ...

Why should I die? ... I am young and I can go away and change my name ... Nobody would know, nobody ... There is still that bread and margarine up there in the yellow tin ... A little of it would keep me alive until the strike was settled some way ... If they found out, I would deny it ... My word is as good as theirs ... But they wouldn't find out until I was gone and they wouldn't know where ... If in after-life I met them and they knew for certain, I would admit it and say I did not think it right to change the object of the strike at the last moment ... One little piece and I could go on for days again ...

But I would know that I had eaten ... Whenever I went that knowledge would be inside me ... the thought of it ... the feel of it ... making me an outcast to myself ... driving me mad ... Everybody would see it, written flamingly all over me, that I had betrayed those who trusted me ... those who scorned to dodge death ... I would want to die then, and I could not ...

I feel colder than I have felt yet ... hands and feet and now up along my legs ... Seems a moving coldness ... Coming towards my heart ... leaving everything it passes over insensible ... Sometimes I have to look at the hump in the blanket to realise that I still have feet ... My hands are that wonderful blue-white, like looking through china ... It isn't the kind of cold that makes you shiver; just the cold of nothing there ... as my teeth felt which were snapped across in that fall ... I can sense it moving upward now ...

I would be glad if this were death coming at last ... It is what they say ... that the heart grows weaker and weaker and merely stops ... It is too weak now to send the blood far ... To be calm for the end and like this is great happiness ... Wish the Governor was here now ... It would be delicious just to smile up at him and keep smiling as the light slowly died out of the eyes and the life out of the face ... and not cease to smile ... To say cheerily at the last: 'Well, good-bye now; we have no enmity for you,

Governor, at all; you are just as much a victim of a vicious system as we are. Good-bye.'

The little man would be dreadfully upset about it all … But I wouldn't like a crowd of people to be standing round as I died … even people I know and like … I could say nothing … It would be like being seen off at a station with a crowd round the carriage door after all the farewells were spoken … Some of the people watching me would sob or ask silly questions and be snarled at by others … I can understand an old person dying with his family about him … But old people, they say, are glad to go, and their time for going is not an unfair time … They have spent their lives … Their lives aren't snatched from them …

The alternating calmness and raving seems to be what O'Sullivan talked so much of … 'The double personality' … One half of me wants to die, wisely wants to die, knowing with such clear knowledge that life *is* empty and the world is empty and friendships are empty; and it is a divine kindness which gives a man a chance of going out of life for about the one thing that does matter … Death appears powerless over this personality, to have almost no meaning for it, except a kind of glad meaning as the place where one parts from all the contradictions of life, as the gateway to the inexpressible peace which lies beyond death: the surcease of pain and doubt and desire. This personality perceives that what we do now is not idealism, but the true realism – that nations live by death; that only the dead seed brings forth fruit, and unless dead is barren: that lives given wilfully, thoughtfully, for freedom do create freedom ... At least I can say that if I am afraid of death, all of me is not ...

The other half of the double personality seems to be uppermost in me more often ... the fearing, craven part of me. The part of me which is without faith or hope and knows not of charity ... the part that would do any mean trick, tell any lie, adopt any pretence, desert any duty rather than suffer ... the part that has wilful desires and serves them in a hundred treacherous ways ... which hates death, for it has no after-life, or only one of torment ... which rails at death and makes it seem useless and purposeless ... Against the other personality it wages a war in every crisis, a war of fear or of scruples, taking away a man's bodily strength or his spiritual strength ... Like Satan tempting Christ, it uses the arguments of virtue to achieve base ends, and overwhelms its co-dweller with phantoms and fantasies so subtly true and untrue that the mind wastes itself in trying to combat them ...

Yet there seems to be a clear line over which this craven thing cannot reach into ... It may keep the mind from dwelling on the truth; but it cannot change the truth or rob it of its magnetism ... In crises I think it must be powerless, for men die so easily for what is right, so quietly, so happily. The Letters Pearse and the others wrote show how willingly they accepted death, how it was to them not a fearsome, but a lovable, thing ... At such a moment, at the facing of the eternal gateways, the great spirit must take complete possession, crowding out the mean, frightened spirit altogether; making the man a saint even before his time; showing him the unimportance of life, the sweetness of death; perhaps lifting the veil ever so little and filling him with pure desire as a church is filled with incense; perhaps opening his ears to a note or two of the beatific choirs, so that human things become the mysteries and he passes before his killers like a sleep-walker in some sweet dream, with a smile fragile as the bloom of fruit upon his lips and in the depths of his eyes ...

Philip has been here ... Looks very white ... Spoke cheerily, but only to hide his belief that the easy victory is not to be ours after all ... Philip is very game, but he knows now, I think, that the change of winning without deaths is gone ... He would never have been so almost gay unless he had something to hide ... That something was known to both of us, and we spoke without allowing our eyes to meet ...

A blackness has come suddenly upon me ... I am dying,

and damnation is waiting for me ... But there is no escape now but to die ... If I gave in, I could never raise my head again ... Maybe that is what God is asking of me: to yield and be an outcast for ever ... It is too much to ask ... I haven't the strength ...

Everything has lost its meaning except despair ... everything is heavy, heavy, heavy ... There is no sound anywhere except a kind of rushing in the ears ... of black turbulent water ... of horrible, thick, foul water with bodies floating in it, rubbing off the sides of the blackness, so soft that they make no noise even when the pieces break off ... There are a lot of bodies ... going very slowly now ... yet quickening as they go round the bend ... They are not going round the bend now ... the water is choked with them ... Oh! They are standing up ... Horrible wet faces with the flesh slipping off them ... falling into the water ... black splashes ... They are calling 'Coward' at me ... all of them ... with husky whispering voices ... 'Coward, Coward, Coward' ... Others are coming ... whispering too ... 'Human Respect ... Human Respect.' ... They know I am dying for human respect ... There they are, all around me ... Smell from them like iodoform, not a bad smell ... They are looking at me ... Their skulls are coming through their flesh ... Ah! There's Philip ... So Philip is dead ... And Brennan ... His children are there, too, I suppose ... There's the Governor

… They must have killed him … Philip did, I suppose … Horrible the way the flesh peels away from the pressure of his eye-glass … He doesn't seem to mind, though … What are they all waiting for? … They are going to sing … All the jaws hanging loose on their necks … How on earth can they sing like that?

'And that was the last that I saw of my dear.'

That's not the air of it … They are going back into the water … Lying down in it and floating away … There, Philip is gone; the Governor is going down on his hands and knees … Nobody will tell him the right way … 'No speaking with enemy officials' … The rule holds after we are dead, evidently … All the others must be our fellows …

I would be dead, too, if I had really fasted … But I breathed the porridge every morning … I betrayed them all and am alive … The only one of them all … Everybody will know what has kept me alive … They will know that I tricked the others and got them to die first … And now if I am released the crowd outside the gate will jeer and snarl at me … the mothers and wives of the men who died … 'Look at the hunger-striker who had porridge every morning' … They will spit at me and name their dead at me … They will say everywhere that I ate the porridge, although they will know that I only smelt it … Well, let them say it … I won't deny it … How was I to know that we were not to breathe that smell? ... I should have guessed ... I could have blocked up the crevices in the door ... But we were not ordered to ... I obeyed the orders we got ... Yes, the letter, but not the spirit of them ...

Oh! Oh! I wish I had died with the others ... Lord, why didn't You let me? ... Was it because I was not ready to yield if You wanted me too? ... If You had given me the strength I would have been ready ... Now, nobody will understand ... all who looked up to me ... who read what I wrote and thought I meant it ... who were strengthened in facing death by what I had written ... Some of them are dead now ... and the others? How will I tell them so that they will understand that I didn't betray the dead ones wilfully ... didn't run away under fire and shelter behind little boys like Gay and Aiden? ...

I have been lonely and without friends before ... I can be again ... If they think I played false and shamefully, then they don't know me and are not anything to me ... Let them all go their way ... I will not wait on them to explain ... But, oh! it will be an empty, empty life ... God, do let me die ... You let all the others ... I will vow anything if You be merciful to me and let me go also ... Do, God, sweet, kindly God ...

Will they do anything about the Governor, I wonder? ... They surely must do something ... They have started their campaign of assassination ... I remember Tomás

MacCurtain drilling us long ago ... He is dead now ... The stout body of him, I remember it ... They killed him because one of their constables was killed ... A Lord Mayor for a constable ... How many for the Governor of their principal jail? ... That may be why I am living on after all the others ... They will come tonight when it is very dark, very dark and still, just the one light at the top of the ward, silvery gas-light ... They will creep along ... Not the warders, they are friendly ... but the great hulking curs they have everywhere for this work ... They will come ... There are two to be avenged ... Kells as well ... They will blame me for both of them ... But my life will not satisfy them ... They will want more ... But the others are dead ...

Yes, that is why I am living ... They will take their revenge by killing me slowly, by making my death-agony worth the two they have lost ... In the middle of the night they will come ... hoping to find me asleep ... like the man they found sleeping in the raided house and woke to kill that they might enjoy his terror at dying ... They could have killed him asleep; but they would have got no good barrack-room story out of that ... If they torture me I shall go mad ... I know I shall tell them everything ... Oh! if they use fire it will be horrible ... red-hot irons pressed into me ...

That will be their revenge ... They can close the cell-door and nobody will hear me ... They will come in plain clothes and the warders will think they are doctors – coming to cauterise. Ha! Ha! ... special ameliorative treatment ... Ha! Ha! ... I know I will scream and writhe and ... give them their laugh ... The devils must have their laugh, and I won't have the courage not to give it to them ... If I did not scream, they might kill me with an impatient blow; but every cry I make will give them new vigour ... the suppressed everlasting vigour of the torturer ... If I screamed loud enough the people on the canal would hear me ... They would know what it meant; the cry of sudden pain is not like any other cry ... Perhaps somebody, somebody waiting out there for me, somebody who knows me, Aunt Margaret or Nora, would recognise the voice and understand ... But the memory of that cry would then always be with them, an unspeakable memory ... Yet they would know and could tell Celia ...

But the devils will not give me even that chance ... Curfew is on and they will come when the streets are empty ... In the darkness they will come, masked ... I see the big, square bodies of them blocking out the mole-coloured light of the doorway as they enter one by one, stealthily, carrying things hidden under their long coats ... As one prepares the brazier and the other place the iron, one will sit by me and ask, ask, ask. I shall say that I do not know, that I know nothing … And then the smile under the mask and the glow of the iron, and the acrid, hot smell of it coming very near, and the tight grip by the others on my head, and another question and the smell of burning and the pain all together … And then I shall scream and be a coward and go mad and talk and tell them things … I am glad, glad that I do not know who killed the Governor … I shall think of one thing only while they are at me: not to mention the letter 'I am going to Kells tomorrow' … That is all I know that can endanger others who are not dead … If I concentrate on not saying that one thing, I shall not say it, I feel that … But they may be clever and I may have said it before I understand what I am saying … If I do say it, shall ask them to kill me, to torture me as long as they like. I will bear it all if they promise to make sure of me in the end, sure that I am dead before it is found out that it was I who told them …

The people would not even believe that I had to be tortured before I told … They would say that the marks were of some atrocious disease and that I had never been other than a spy … A people can be so cruel; so wantonly, desperately cruel … There seem to be no halves with a people … Either it hates venomously or loves with a kind of delirious abandonment … A man or a cause is lifted up by it and adored … Anything done by the man or the cause is right

... A call, and the people are ready to go to war or death, to immolate themselves, happy that they have been given this chance to express their fidelity ... And then the man is false or the cause becomes corrupt, and the wrath of the people is as hellish as their selflessness was noble ... vile, vixenish hatred for which nothing is too low or too cruel ... It is a dangerous service for the freedom of a people ... Yet not so dangerous; for if the service be sincere the people appear always to understand ... They do not seem to condemn the man who tries and fails, but is ready to try again ... that is if his failure has not been one of principle, a desertion from the tradition ... Sometimes I think there is only one real proof of the sincere worker for an unfreed people ... and that is death ... that until a man has died for his principles the people are not quite sure that he ever held them ... nor is the man himself sure ...

Curious how this line of thought has lifted that awful darkness ... Even the cell seems brighter ... Again I am happy and see clearly the rightfulness of dying in this way ... the joy of dying ... the wonderful, fragrant, holy gift that has been given us ... God, my love, I thank you ... Our nation needs the proof that we and the movement for which we stand are sincere, that the doctrine we preach is the true national doctrine, and we, with the loving grace of God, are going joyfully to give them proof ... Oh! I am so proud, with such a happiness in me, surging in me, thrilling though me, lifting me up, so it seems, up, up, until a gladness not of this world is in my heart, and a knowledge and surety not of this world is in my mind and my soul that what we do is godly and perfect, and by it our people shall become free … There are no words to speak this exaltation … I shall go to Philip and tell him how right he has been …

# Wednesday, April 14th, 1920: 8.30 p.m.

It is all over! ... The strike is over! ... We have won! I think I was sorry when I heard it ... now I am glad, glad that we have not failed and that we are to live ... It is a different kind of happiness from that of giving up life willingly, but it is real too ... That other rapture, this has something more robust and genial in it, more physical, perhaps ... The thought of winning the strike and keeping our lives came to me often, and the anticipation of such a victory was delicious ... The reality seems limp; but it may only be the reaction ... I didn't understand at first what Philip was saying ...

As I left the cell to tell him that he was right, I remembered that he was dead ... that I had seen him dead, him and the Governor ... I held on to the wire-caging to think it out, and then noticed others at their cell doors also ... waiting for something ... I thought they had come out to watch me; that they were all dead and were jealously watching my cell for me to come from it, dead also … I saw them turn my way at the noise of my movements … I lowered my head not to see their faces, and was edging back into my cell when … Down below there was a murmur … running feet in light shoes … I saw O'Kelly, the warder, rush up the iron stairs two at a time, say something to the man at the cell-door nearest the stairs, and then run to Philip's cell … Without any effort of my will or memory everything became real; the ghosts were men, I knew their names and Christian names. Philip was alive; the Governor, too … The strength of excitement was in me and I almost ran to the end of the stairs … I heard Philip shout and did not understand … The men at their doors cheered, really cheered, meaning it … Philip took my hand when I went into the cell …

'They've given in, Frank,' he said, 'We're all going home.'

The warder was there, smiling broadly … While I was thinking out what Philip had told me, O'Kelly explained: 'Governor just back from the Viceregal: I was outside the office and heard him say to the Deputy: "It's settled; they're to be released".'

Talked to Philip after O'Kelly had gone … Have no recollection of what we said, except that we laughed a lot, which made me ask him about the girls who had gone through the passage laughing ... He didn't see them, but said he could hear girls outside, laughing evidently in the crowd outside the gates, joyously happy that the strike, as they thought then, was over ... Don't like to ask any others for fear it was only ... only that ...

The official settlement of the strike is the usual face-saving compromise of a defeated tyrant ... The Governor came to Philip and said: 'The Government cannot change its decision; your men can be released only on parole.'

I can imagine how hard Philip's face became.

'We can't give parole,' Philip said, his eyes narrowed and his chin forward. 'What's your game in playing with us like this?'

The Governor then explained that his Government did not need a written parole; that they would take the acceptance by each man of his release as his acceptance of parole.

'Then no man will accept his release,' said Philip.

'Oh! but you'll have to go,' the Governor replied, and turned to leave me cell.

'Look here,' Philip called after him, 'Will you inform your authorities that we refuse to give any written, verbal or implied parole; that we are not coming back at the end of six weeks or any other time; and if, in spite of this declaration, your authorities still release us, we shall accept that release as absolutely unconditional?' ...

And the Governor went away looking more worn than ever …

It is almost nine o'clock and there has been no release yet … Nobody is to eat until he is outside the gate, free … The men have also been told that they must give no understanding of any sort to come back again …

The jail has become a different world in less than an hour … There is laughter in every cell and a snatch of a song here and there … and the hum of talk about the things that will be done and said tomorrow … In the cell next to me there are four men playing bridge … I can hear the calling …

Was round to Peter Starkey's cell and overheard a tremendous plan for a steak-and-chips supper tonight. Peter Starkey is wanted for the rest of the war, so Philip and I have arranged with the doctor that all men go either to a home where they will be properly nursed or to hospital … There are a hundred beds ready at the Mater, the warders say …

Wonder what the delay is? … If the whole thing broke down again and the strike had to be resumed, it would break us, body and spirit … But it won't … We have won, very definitely; or rather the people outside have won … Tomorrow we shall be sipping warm drinks at home … joy!

Ah! It has begun ... We are to be released singly ... They have called for Aiden ... Glad he's the first: a mere kid with the courage of a lion ... Seems to be some ceremony about the business ... There is a little group of officials down in the circle ... the Governor, the doctor, Hartnett, the head-warder ... The Governor has something in his hand like a bundle of papers ... He is reading something over to Aiden ... The half-light, the distance, the bars of the wing gates make it difficult to see ... If each release takes as long as Aiden's, we shall be here some time ...

Nine o'clock ... Four have gone out already ... Three in stretchers ... Sent a note to the doctor to get Brennan taken next, as he has collapsed again ... He looked gruesome there on the floor, with his white, white face and his eyes closed and just a touch of froth at the corners of his blue-lipped mouth ... He is more wasted than any of the others ... Noticed this throat as he lay there, like the corded throat of an old, old woman ... The strain of this waiting is too great for most of us ... If they would only take the names alphabetically, some could go back to bed ...

Ten o'clock ... Thirty-five have gone ... Philip went off just after nine and Twomey a few minutes ago ... Some of us will surely be left over till the morning ... Fitz* will be outside and Erskine, too, perhaps ... Unless I am called

*Fitz was the late Anna Kelly (born Fitzsimons) who was a well-known Republican and journalist.

soon they will go away ... If they left us overnight there might be new conditions that we could not accept ... The General Strike will have been called off ... We have divided our forces foolishly ... all should have gone out together ... It may be a trap ... to hold a few of us for victimisation ... There's Gay off ... 'So long, Gay; tell them outside we're coming soon; to hold on.' He looks stronger than he did last Sunday ... A lot of the seemingly strongest men went to pieces when the word of release came, and some of the weak ones got back their strength ... I don't understand how this hunger-striking works, but its ways are curious ...

Eleven o'clock ... The name-calling goes on and on and ... no sound of mine ... The Governor down there has put on his overcoat ... My heart jumped at first; I thought he was going away ... The doctor is walking up and down, but the Governor stands his ground like a well-trained soldier ... He must be frozen ... Fifty-nine gone now ... More stretcher cases ... The appalling tension of listening avariciously for one's name has led to many collapses ... All but four of those who went out since ten o'clock had to be carried out ... It is bitterly cold too ... The jail becomes eerie and a mad place without the sounds of men ... like a house in which a dead body is, where nobody speaks above a whisper and everybody walks on tip-toe ... Every stone in the jail, every stone is becoming hateful to me ... To while away the time men form themselves into little groups and gather in one cell: then one and another of the group goes … and longing descends upon the others, and the fear, like a cold hand on the pit of the stomach, of being forgotten … A score of times I have felt that my name has been passed over by accident … That when the Governor reached my name somebody said: 'Oh! He's gone', and that they won't discover it until Curfew is on and it is too late to go … The thought of one more night here is worse than the whole ten days we have passed through …

Now that I know I am to be released, I cannot rest, not one second, until I am out of here … They may send me to hospital … I shall cry if they do … to be in a ward, to see and hear other men about you, the same men of the last ten days, to hear them talk, talk of the hunger-strike, surely that would complete my madness … I want to be away from it all … To be where there is nobody … to be utterly and absolutely alone … In a bright room … a bright room with a soft white-sheeted bed … and with flowers … yes, with flowers … and a fire … To sleep there when I will … or to remain awake and not have to talk … to look at the flowers and stir the fire … and think … and smile to myself … I want it so much, so ravenously, that it can hardly happen … I will tell the matron of whatever hospital they bring me to that I won't stay … that I won't break my fast until she lets me out of the place ... That ... that I will go back to the jail and stay here ... The smell of a hospital would kill me ... I know ...

'Yes, David, what is it? Are you going? ... *My* name?'

*'Frank Gallagher.'*

'Coming!'

*'Frank Gallagher.'*

'Damn it, man, I'm coming' ...

## Midnight, April 14th, 1920

The taxi-driver would not take his fare ... He said he would be proud all his life that he had driven one of us ... Everywhere the same feeling ... We drove out from the jail and the car had to run through an avenue of people half a mile long standing there still, after four hours' rain ... The umbrellas with the street lights shining on them ... and the same light reflected by the drenched shoulders and caps of many young men who had no overcoats ... Little things that show how moved the people are ...

As I reached the circle after my name was called, I realised that two warders were helping me ... Must have fallen on the way down, for I cannot remember their coming to me ... The Governor looked like a very old parrot: just as sad-looking and as old-looking and as frail-looking ... The collar of his overcoat was not properly straightened out — evidence of supreme weariness in this dapper little man

... He wore no hat ... The helping warders brought me opposite him and he started reading from a slip of paper, his staccato voice sounding very low and mechanical ... Guessed this had something to do with the parole we would not give, so I turned to talk to the doctor, feeling a pang that I should be discourteous to so tired and well-meaning a Governor ... Told the doctor I felt very fit and was going home to be nursed ... He nodded and smiled as I turned back to the Governor, who had ceased reading.

'You know I am not coming back,' I said. 'Good-bye.'

'Good-bye and good luck,' he said.

We shook hands ... Forgetting the two warders, I ran out through the narrow hall on to the front steps ... Heard my name called ... Kissed somebody ... shook hands evidently stretched for that purpose ... Heard Lt Millar's voice: 'Up, K Company!' and more dimly the voices of other Volunteers I knew ... Realised that the main gates had swung open and that I was in a taxi passing through them ... Conscious that Fitz's eyes were very bright and that I was leaning back on a white pillow ... Saw faces close to the windows on each side of the taxi ... Watched a rain-drop gather others on the way and with a sudden little run meet the wood frame of the glass ... Heard somebody call for cheers: then a 'Sh-sh-sh! ... Sick man' ... And suddenly the crowd becoming very still ... As the car moved slowly through the people, I heard a young girl ask softly: 'Who is it, Mister?' and immediately, 'Oh! he's dying ... The priest is with him' ... I had not noticed until then that Denis was with us ... And now we were out of the crowds and the streets looked bare and lonely ... The tram-tracks were lines of platinum under the purple-white light of the arclamps ... Saw a covered car reflected in the rain-polished pavement ...

Fitz said we would get it here and the taxi slowed down and stopped ... An argument at the door ... 'Could not ... it's long after hours' ... It was a public-house ... 'No, sir,' repeated the landlord. 'It is long after hours' ... Silence, and then the landlord's voice again in surprised tones: 'One of the hunger-strikers, is it? Why didn't you tell me? Here, sir,' and he offered me the wine-glass of brandy himself ... He seemed disappointed when he heard my name ... Evidently I was not one of the mighty ones ... However, it would make a good story in the bar next day ... all the better for a change of name ...

The brandy tingled in my toes and along my scalp ... Inside, there was five minutes of sheer physical joy ... warmth, spreading out like water on a blotter, fragrance, a sense of luxurious ease ... a kind of unbreakable repose ... And then I started to talk ... and to laugh ...

I sit by a fire now ... and there are flowers here ... and the pillows, and even the coverlet, are white, white ...

# AFTER DAWN, THURSDAY, APRIL 15TH, 1920

If I open my eyes again and that square window is there
still ... and the flowers and trees! ... But if they are not
there ... that will break my heart ... The jail windows are
small and semicircular, and the bars and mulled glass keep
out the light ... And my cell window was at the foot of my
bed and this is at the side ... the last time I looked at it I
saw it at the side ... large and square and with a green casement ... I saw it ... I am sure I saw it ... I could not have
dreamt it so clearly ... I hear the birds singing now ... That
is a thrush ... and a blackbird too ... I never heard birds in
my cell, except pigeons in the eaves ... I smell the earth ...
I never smelt the earth in my cell ...

As long as I do not open my eyes I can have my dream;
and even if there is a doubt, it is better than knowing for
certain ... The bed feels different ... God, You wouldn't
be as cruel as that ... It is ... it must be real ... I hear the

birds again … Jesus, let it be true … give me strength to look … to look and know … I'll bear it for Your sake if it isn't so … A square window … I saw that … clear glass in it … two panes … green, green trees and shrubs and grass outside … Yes, thrush I'll look now … just now … give me a minute more and I'll look …

A square window … green trees … a blue, blue sky … and such sweet birds. It is true … I want to sing too.

# Other books from Mercier Press

## Blood on the Streets

*1916 & the Battle for Mount Street Bridge*

## Paul O'Brien

ISBN: 978 1 85635 576 6

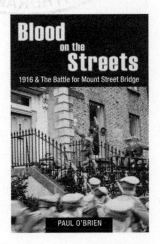

26 April 1916: a small band of Volunteers killed or wounded 240 British soldiers before they were overpowered and defeated in the bloodiest battle of the Rising.

*Blood on the Streets* explores what really happened during the battle for Mount Street Bridge. Based around the bridge over the canal at Mount Street, three well-positioned groups of Volunteers led by Lieutenant Michael Malone held out against a far greater number of British soldiers arriving from Dún Laoghaire. In scenes that were reminiscent of the terrible warfare of the Western Front in the First World War, British soldiers advanced under heavy fire against rebel positions.

This book examines this battle and other events surrounding the Rising, and features the only written account by a British army officer of the executions at Kilmainham jail in the aftermath of the Rising.

# The Burning of Cork

Brendan O'Shea and Gerry White

ISBN: 978 1 85635 522 3

On the night of 11 December 1920, Cork City experienced an orgy of unprecedented terror at the hands of the British forces of law and order. The War of Independence was in its second year and the previous nine months had witnessed a dramatic escalation of the conflict.

In Cork, attacks on the crown forces by the Irish Volunteers were being answered with vicious reprisals, and the streets had become the battleground of a bloody and personalised war of attrition.

With two lord mayors dead, several British officers either kidnapped or assassinated, and tension increasing on a daily basis, the fuse had been lit for a night of violence and arson that the people of Cork city would never forget ...